Praise for *The (Practically) Perfect Teacher*

Jackie Beere has the great skill of making links between some complex ideas of research and theory and the practical reality of daily life in the classroom. Her book resonates with images that teachers will recognise as things that happen with pupils in the everyday quest for learning. She offers step-by-step advice and suggestions that are tailored in a way that can be used tomorrow. The advice is built upon sound research that is explained and grounded to make it accessible. This wisdom is then trained on the pressures that teachers find themselves under and the excitement of the job.

Jackie has produced an engaging book, full of a passionate belief in the satisfaction to be gained from the professional job of teaching. The book oozes with sense, techniques to try and the joy of seeing young people learning.

Mick Waters, Professor of Education, Wolverhampton University

In an ever-changing educational context, *The Practically Perfect Teacher* passionately inspires and energises by explicitly highlighting the key habits of an effective teacher. Through her reader-friendly style, Jackie Beere enables the reader to combine the notions of self-belief and a fervent desire to succeed along with a child-centred approach to provide practical strategies for all teachers seeking to deliver impact and make a positive difference to the lives of children!

**Haroon Asghar, Deputy Head Teacher,
Brookhouse Community Primary School**

The book is packed with honest, down-to-earth ways we can all make the learning journey of young people more worthwhile and memorable: from theory which challenges long-held beliefs to classroom practice ideas that reinforce what is expected of outstanding teachers. The book is bound to stimulate staffroom debate and motivate teachers to reflect on their practice. Nothing the book suggests is budget-breaking or beyond the reach of any school, and we will certainly be using most of the teaching strategies and ideas suggested. In fact, we can't wait to get started!

I found it really easy to read – quite a page turner – and as a true lifelong learner I wanted to find out more!

Much of the book reaffirms my beliefs about teaching; however, every chapter has those 'little gems' that can make a huge difference to any school. I will certainly put it on the essential reading list of every teacher in my school. As always, Jackie's top tips are superb school-improvement ideas in a nutshell.

Beverley Dandy, Head Teacher, Outwoods Primary School

A concise and engaging book which focuses on the teacher and their impact on students. This is a book which explores why teachers teach and how they can improve how they teach. This is a book for anyone involved in education; although many of the examples have a school context, the principles apply to all those tasked with developing understanding and knowledge in others. This book is ideal for experienced teachers seeking motivation, reinvigoration or simply a fresh perspective but may also prove highly beneficial for those seeking pearls of wisdom at the start of their career.

Drawing on a wealth of experience and research, the author outlines a framework for continual self-development, driven not by external quality procedures but a desire to maximise the achievement and personal development of the students. The book includes practices and rituals to develop student-focused teachers, driven by feedback in which the teacher is reflective, adaptive and innovative. There is a strong focus on the student as a partner in the educational process, influencing their teaching through feedback, and engaging with the teacher and their peers to develop both academically and as an individual. As a university lecturer, I see the development of students as independent learners, who are engaged and enthusiastic about education, as an essential component of teaching.

Dr Glenn Jenkins, Lecturer, University of Wales Trinity St. David:
Swansea Metropolitan

At a time when the pressure on teachers is greater than it ever has been, Jackie reminds us why we chose this wonderful profession and of the enormous difference we can make to the lives of the children we teach. Not only is this book packed with practical ideas that you can apply in your classroom immediately, it will also challenge you to step back and take a much closer look at the unconscious habits, attitudes and values that ultimately determine how effective you are as a teacher.

Whilst there is no guarantee that reading this book will make you the 'perfect teacher', it will certainly help you to become the best teacher you can possibly be, and who can ask for more than that?

James Bowen, Head Teacher, Mill Rythe Junior School

After reading *The Practically Perfect Teacher* I can't wait to try out some of Jackie's ideas! I believe, as teachers, we are always striving to be the very best we can but are never satisfied with any of our achievements – always feeling we can do that bit better. Hopefully with the advice and guidance from this book we can ultimately achieve our goal.

Leisha Champion BA (Hons) PGCE,
Fourlanesend Community Primary School

I am so pleased to have read this uplifting book which reminded me that I have the best job in the world! A term of teaching can leave you feeling weary, stressed out and counting the 'wake-ups' until the next break. However, after reading this book, I could not wait to get back into class to try out some new techniques, ideas and 'mindset tweaks'.

I have already implemented the 3B4ME and my class suggestions board is teeming with feedback from pupils who are taking control of their own learning. I had a smile on my face all day long when a usually reticent pupil excitedly filled in a sticky note for the suggestions board and explained a starter activity which he had devised to improve our learning!

I feel I am being a lot more honest with my pupils, explaining that the 'learning zone' is not a 'comfort zone' but will be challenging, frustrating and even painful at times. My class are also embracing more fully the concept that every mistake is a learning experience.

This book has encouraged me to reflect more honestly on my teaching, but not to beat myself up when something hasn't gone to plan. Instead, I am embracing the fact that there is no such thing as failure, only a part of the journey towards success!

Sue Ware, KS2 Teacher, The King John School

Jackie is forever inspiring, both in how she presents and in what she has to say. I think this book is her best yet! It's an amazing book. Normally education-based books can be dry and uninspiring. This book, however, is very well written and presented. I could not put it down! The book is a concise approach to quality first teaching and learning, with a huge emphasis on the learning. It is great how it reflects on Ofsted and the criteria for good learning. It's a must-read for all teachers old and new! I certainly will be ordering copies for my staff!

Shane Jarman, Head Teacher, Denaby Main Primary School

This is the third of Jackie's books I have read, and she continues to summarise a complex profession, whilst allowing for the necessary individual approach, in a short helpful and easy-to-read form. There is a danger with any book that claims to help someone become the 'perfect' teacher that the advice will be patronising, impractical and easily misunderstood. Jackie overcomes all these hurdles by ensuring an up-to-date knowledge of the demands of teaching through practical involvement and extensive research. At no point does Jackie take it for granted that teachers have excess time for preparation as all hints and tips are quick to read and translate into the classroom. This book is for any teacher, whatever their experience and subject. There is genuinely something new and useful to help every lesson progress with high levels of pupil engagement and challenge.

Hannah Horwood, Assistant Head (Teaching and Learning),
Surbiton High School

THE PERFECT TEACHER

PRACTICALLY

Jackie Beere

Independent Thinking Press

First published by
Independent Thinking Press
Crown Buildings, Bancyfelin, Carmarthen, Wales, SA33 5ND, UK
www.independentthinkingpress.com

Independent Thinking Press is an imprint of Crown House Publishing Ltd.

First published 2014

Illustration p. 123 © Matthew Cole and Irina Onufrieva – fotolia.com
Illustration p. 127 © Dmitriy Shpilko, Zsolt Fulop and Gouraud Studio – fotolia.com

Quotes from Government documents used in this publication have
been approved under an Open Government Licence.
Please visit www.nationalarchives.gov.uk/doc/open-government-licence/

British Library Cataloguing-in-Publication Data
A catalogue entry for this book is available
from the British Library.

Edited by John Beasley

Print ISBN 978-178135100-0
Mobi ISBN 978-178135139-0
ePub ISBN 978-178135140-6

Printed and bound in the UK by
Gomer Press, Llandysul, Ceredigion

This book is dedicated to our grandchildren. Dearest Jack, who lived for such a brief moment, and the beautiful Lyla Elizabeth, who brings so much pleasure every day.

May the next generation of young learners enjoy an education that inspires and fulfils them ... and may they meet teachers who absolutely love their jobs.

Contents

Acknowledgements

I would like to thank all the wonderful teachers and school leaders who I have had the pleasure of working with over the past few years. Their determination to make a difference and their enthusiasm for learning how has been the inspiration for this book. A special thanks to all those who welcomed me into their school to train or observe; each and every time I work with teachers I learn something new.

Introduction

The quality of a country's education system cannot exceed the quality of its teachers.

Michael Barber and Mona Mourshed[1]

All the evidence shows that the most valuable assets of any successful school are the teachers, delivering lessons to children every day. We cannot underestimate the power and influence of a great teacher in the life of a child. No matter what changes are made to systems or to the curriculum or inspection regimes, one certainty remains: children will be helped or hindered in their progress, learning, self-esteem, qualifications, job prospects, life chances and, indeed, happiness by the teachers they come across over their 13 years in the education system. So teaching is still a wonderful, powerful, vitally important job, despite the uncertainty created by changing political currents.

This book aims to consider how to be the very best teacher you can be, not just for Ofsted or for your line manager, but for the kids – because there is nothing better than delivering great lessons that inspire them. Helping youngsters, for

---

1 M. Barber and M. Mourshed, *How the World's Best Performing School Systems Come Out On Top* (London: McKinsey & Company, 2007), p. 13.

whom you may be the only hope, to develop a motivation to learn and encouraging them to experience the excitement of achieving great results is life-changing stuff and worth getting up for. However, it is hard work – harder than ever – and the expectations that you will deliver are very high, so you need to be made of stern stuff to be a teacher. You have to be the ultimate lifelong learner, willing to reflect, self-evaluate, adapt, be eternally optimistic and massively determined to make a difference for *all* your pupils – even those who push your buttons! There will be times in your career when it won't seem worth it or when it all goes wrong. However, if you can learn from this then you will be a better teacher for it. I have found inspiration from a speech given by J. K. Rowling to Harvard University alumni where she celebrates the strength and resilience created by making mistakes and surviving adversity:

> Failure gave me an inner security that I had never attained by passing examinations. Failure taught me things about myself that I could have learned no other way.[2]

Teaching is a profession where you never stop learning from your mistakes or wondering what else you can do to inspire, intrigue, motivate or mesmerise your classes. The challenge is

---

2 J. K. Rowling, 'The Fringe Benefits of Failure and the Importance of Imagination'. Commencement Address at the 2008 Annual Meeting of the Harvard Alumni Association.

on for our 21st century schools. We need to develop 'learning that is irresistible', as Mick Waters so aptly describes in *Thinking Allowed on Schooling*[3] – and avoid being tempted by shortcuts that make a quick-fix impact on exam results but fail to develop great learners who can confidently compete for jobs in a global marketplace.

This book doesn't cover everything you need to be a 'perfect' teacher (there is no such thing, of course), but it points the way along that eternal learning journey to be the very best you can be – so that you can help your pupils be the very best they can be.

And then that will be the very best job you could ever have.

---

3   M. Waters, *Thinking Allowed on Schooling* (Carmarthen: Independent Thinking Press, 2013), p. 290.

Chapter 1

Framing your mind –
thinking on purpose

Do you love your job? For at least 70% of the week? Do you wake up on a school-week Monday morning excited and enthusiastic about the challenges the week will bring? Are you energised by the thought of finding a way, at last, to turn your most recalcitrant pupil on to learning?

However, on a rainy Friday afternoon at the end of a long hard term, when the class seem oblivious to how you tried to make it interesting and fun because they prefer texting love messages, interrupting the lesson by shouting obscenities or just gazing longingly at the door and waiting for the bell, it's bloody hard! If you don't feel useless and challenged some of the time, you will never have the motivation to find new strategies that could turn that difficult class around. It's not what happens to you, it's how you respond to it that will matter as a teacher – and how you respond depends on how you think about things. This chapter will help you discover how to have the mindset that will help you be the best teacher you can be. And yes, it is a choice. Decide now that you will suspend disbelief and take control of your thinking.

It will help you to be a better teacher and, as a side benefit, it will help every other aspect of your life.

In John Hattie's seminal work *Visible Learning for Teachers*,[1] he argues that the most successful teachers and school leaders believe that they are 'agents of change' and work in schools that nurture this way of thinking in their teachers. Hattie outlines eight mindframes teachers and leaders have which maximise impact on learning in schools:

Teachers/leaders:

1. Believe that their core task is to evaluate the effect of their teaching.

2. Believe that success and failure in student learning is about what *they* did or did not do.

3. Want to talk more about the learning than the teaching.

4. See assessment as feedback about the impact of their teaching.

5. Engage in dialogue with their students and *listen* to them.

6. Enjoy the challenge and avoid making excuses or just 'doing their best'.

---

1 J. Hattie, *Visible Learning for Teachers: Maximizing Impact on Learning* (London: Routledge, 2012).

7. Believe that it is their role to develop positive relationships in classrooms/staffrooms.

8. Inform all about the language of learning.

Make no mistake: the way you think makes you the teacher that you are. After research based on 800 meta-analyses of 50,000 articles with 150,000 effect sizes and 240 million students, Hattie drew some crucial conclusions based on nurturing beliefs and values that impact on our thinking. He believes that how we think in schools constitutes 'a set of principles that create mindframes to underpin our every action and decision'.[2] It is a belief that we are evaluators, change agents, adaptive learning experts and seekers of feedback about our impact, engaged in dialogue and challenge about learning. To be really effective in our role we see opportunity in error and are keen to spread the message about how powerful we can be as teachers and the impact that we have on learning. It is encouraging to realise that the most important aspect of being a great teacher is the way you think about your job! This is something we can all master by being determined to think purposefully in the way that works to make you the best teacher you can be.

---

2   Hattie, *Visible Learning for Teachers*, p. 159.

So, what are the habits and behaviours of the most succesful teachers? A quick survey of teachers on Twitter produced this Wordle:

So where do all of these essential behaviours of the very best teachers come from? We all hold fundamental principles and beliefs, out of which come the values we believe to be important. From these, in turn, emerge our mindframes or mindsets (the ways in which we unconsciously think about the world and which affect our attitudes and actions). These attitudes and actions can then, in turn, become unconscious (but visible) habits and personality traits that can have a positive or negative effect on our performance.

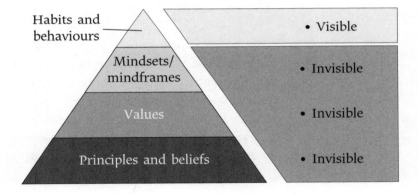

We can, however, deliberately nurture positive, or growth, mindsets – and this is what this chapter is about. Metacognition: thinking on purpose about the way we think and see the world.

Frame your mind – using metacognition

> *Watch your thoughts, for they become words.*
>
> *Watch your words, for they become actions.*
>
> *Watch your actions, for they become habits.*
>
> *Watch your habits, for they become character.*
>
> *Watch your character, for it becomes your destiny.*
>
> Anonymous

Never underestimate the power of the principles, beliefs and values that rule your life because they constantly work away on your unconscious mind, creating thoughts, inner dialogue, vocabulary, behaviours, attitudes and sometimes fixed, inflexible mindsets that define who you are. Once they are fixed, or habitual, you don't even know they are there – but they form your personality and preferences, driving your unconscious mind to make choices and decisions.

Consider these statements (or ones more appropriate to you) and examine the beliefs that feed them, grow them and make them become a reality that is fixed. Challenge your fixed mindsets with questions like, 'Why am I thinking like that? and 'How could I change that?'

- I'm not really into computers.
- Meeting new people makes me nervous.
- I've never been good at maths.

- I wouldn't dance at a party – let alone for the school panto.
- I'm always late – it's in my genes!
- I would never drive in London.
- I always panic during a lesson observation.
- Eating in company makes me nervous.
- I never want to stand up and speak in public.

> By monitoring the micro patterns of activity in the frontopolar cortex, the researchers [at the Max Planck Institute for Human Cognitive and Brain Sciences] could predict which hand the participant would choose 7 seconds before the participant was aware of the decision.[3]

Our unconscious mind puts our own perceptual frame around everything we experience:

---

3   See http://exploringthemind.com/the-mind/brain-scans-can-reveal-your-decisions-7-seconds-before-you-decide (accessed 10 September 2013).

Do you see the good or the evil? Can you switch back and forth easily? What about that difficult boy in your class – do you see him as sparky and interesting or annoying and nasty? If you are going to an important interview do you find yourself rehearsing an inner dialogue along the lines of, 'Well, I probably won't get it', 'My mind is gonna go blank', 'They won't like me'?

Metacognition means metaphorically standing back from these thoughts and wondering where they come from and if you can change them. Thinking on purpose, rather than in a random, unmonitored way, can help you change your mindset more easily when you need to. Being able to do this can be very powerful, especially for teachers under pressure to perform.

It's easy for teachers to get into the habit of blaming the kids or the parents or ourselves when something goes wrong, stereotyping certain kinds of learners or, by default setting, moaning in the staffroom. Habits start off as a choice, like arriving early, sitting in that same chair in the staffroom or choosing to moan, but once they become automatic (habitual) we don't even realise that this is what we do – unless we metacognitively step back from ourselves.

Charles Duhigg, in his book *The Power of Habit*, examined the neuroscience of habit and made a compelling case for acknowledging and challenging our default settings:

> Then we stopped making a choice and the behaviour became automatic. It's a natural consequence of our neurology. And by understanding how it happens, you can rebuild those patterns in whichever way you choose.[4]

Taking control – using metacognition

The very best teachers have great habits for learning and nurture those habits in their learners. This section is about how to take control of your thinking habits so that you can be the teacher you want to be. Andrew Curran studied millions of dollars' worth of research about the human brain and concluded:

> [Our] unique human ability [is] to be able to turn our thoughts inwards and observe ourselves and our own mental life. This is an extraordinarily powerful observation because it is only through this ability that you can understand your own emotions and hence the emotions of others.[5]

---

4   C. Duhigg, *The Power of Habit: Why We Do What We Do and How to Change* (London: William Heinemann, 2012), p. xvii.
5   A. Curran, *The Little Book of Big Stuff about the Brain* (Carmarthen: Crown House Publishing, 2008), p. 22.

So, self-evaluating your own thoughts and actions is vital to becoming the best teacher you can be, because to be outstanding, teachers constantly think about, then adapt and tweak their practice until it works! Outstanding teachers embrace challenge and change and constantly model how to cope with them for their pupils. As Carol Dweck observes:

> [G]reat teachers believe in the growth of the intellect and talent, and they are fascinated with the process of learning.[6]

Dweck's decades of psychological research work creates a powerful argument for the importance of approaching our goals with a growth rather than a fixed mindset. Stephen Covey's seminal work on the habits of successful people has also inspired generations to consider how they can think differently to create better outcomes:

> By consistently applying the principles contained in these habits, you can bring about positive changes in any relationship or situation. You can become an agent of change.[7]

---

6 C. Dweck, *Mindset: The New Psychology of Success* (New York: Random House, 2006), p. 194.
7 S. R. Covey, *The 7 Habits of Highly Effective Families* (London: Simon & Schuster, 1998), p. 17.

This book takes Dweck's and Covey's research and links it to Hattie's mindframes to create seven key mindsets.

The seven mindsets

Remind yourself of these mindsets frequently – until they sink into your unconscious and become part of who you are. They will become the bedrock for your teaching and motivate you throughout your career:

Believe you can
make a difference

Self-evaluate

Use a
language of
learning

Collaborate
to grow

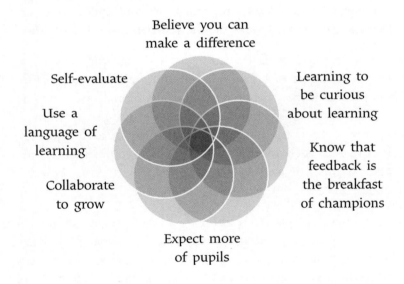

Learning to
be curious
about learning

Know that
feedback is
the breakfast
of champions

Expect more
of pupils

Mindset 1: Self-evaluate

Know yourself – know your impact: 'I know what difference I am making to my pupils and why it works or doesn't work'

Do you have your own process of self-evaluation that helps you adjust your teaching so that it works more effectively every day? All schools must have a self-evaluation process that reflects their performance. You need to replicate this in microcosm with your own ongoing self-evaluation process – measuring your success, reflecting on your judgements and planning your next move on the journey towards brilliance.

'Know thy impact' is the strongest message that Hattie has for us, in terms of knowing what will make the most difference to our learners.[8] Not just in terms of long-term outcomes – exam results, levels and test results – but also in terms of getting wise to the effect you are having in each and every lesson, with each and every pupil, so that you can amend and address this if it isn't working. Common sense? So, how is it done?

First, develop your intuition – never underestimate gut instinct. Get your antennae out, detecting what is and isn't working. The more you use intuition the better it will work. Why did that lesson go well? How did that student do on that task? What feedback can I give the quiet, clever boy who never does much? Second, seek feedback about how progress is going with different learners. Listen to comments and conversations, look at body language and facial expressions, and

---

8   Hattie, *Visible Learning for Teachers*, p. ix.

notice the work they are producing during the lesson. Finally, connect all of these together so that you can quickly assimilate at all times how children are progressing. All of this is rich intelligence that will give you vital clues about your impact.

So, what other feedback is available to you in your classroom? What students say in answer to questions and discussions, how they sit, how hard they work, how often they give you feedback, what their parents say, whether they attend, how punctual they are to your lessons, whether they do your homework or ask you how you are, and how they ask you the classic question, 'What are we doing today, Miss?' Tune in to their behaviour so that you can honestly evaluate how your teaching is going. Get curious about why some lessons or strategies work and others don't.

I'd no idea that changing the seating arrangement would be so challenging for them.

That's interesting – she's never worked that hard. What am I doing right today?

Exactly what *does* my class need to do next to make good progress? What extra help will Emma need, and what can I give Josh that will ensure he is fully challenged?

The (Practically) Perfect Teacher

Learning log notes: Tuesday. Maths. Year 6

Plus	Minus	Interesting
Prompt start	Board game starter took too long	Work finished very quickly
Groups worked well	Ben distracted	New feedback/response policy is working for half the pupils
Murat made outstanding progress	Pace led to messy presentation	Sent early finishers outside to find examples of angles – brilliant outcomes
Plenary really nailed progress through success criteria	Forgot homework	

18

The most important thing about feedback is that you *do* something about it. You adjust and adapt on a minute-to-minute, hourly, daily and weekly basis. You make mistakes, take advice, discuss, share with colleagues and try something different. It is an iterative process and a continuous learning experience. Keep a note of plus, minus and interesting stuff about each lesson, week and term. This can be a rough mind-map or observations in a notebook, on your phone, tablet or in a more formal portfolio. It doesn't even matter if you never read them again; simply the act of writing it down will help you evaluate, synthesise and act on your conclusions. Your notes could eventually become a teacher's blog or book, and will certainly be a very useful and amusing reference in years to come.

This mindset of self-evaluation will inevitably lead you to action research projects which you can share with your colleagues. They don't have to be major academic experiments in controlled conditions, but simple, small-scale adventures into assessing what works and what doesn't.

How did I get Stephen to produce more written work?

I had been experimenting with using music to inspire my Year 11 English bottom set and discovered that nothing pleased everyone, so I was about to give up. However, I noticed that my most challenging student, Stephen, who couldn't sit still, let alone focus enough to write for 40 minutes, seemed much calmer with music on, so I allowed him to plug himself in to his own choice of music and write an essay under controlled conditions for coursework.

He sat and wrote quietly and industriously. I was amazed when I saw that he produced more complex sentences, better handwriting and quality analysis at least two grades superior to anything he had done before. I was intrigued to listen in on his headphones and was shocked to hear screamingly loud dance trance music – a horrible noise. But it worked for him and his essay reflected his true ability. I shared this with colleagues and used the technique again as a brain distractor with students with attention deficit hyperactivity disorder (ADHD) – with lots of positive anecdotal feedback about outcomes.

A self-evaluative mindset demands a relentless curiosity about finding new ways to turn on the brains of your pupils, meaning we will always be learning about learning. Keep up to date with the latest research that may inform your practice by scanning through the teacher's press and the Twitter teaching community where you can link up with teachers' blogs about their current practice and join in discussion forums. This is a truly invaluable continuing professional development (CPD) tool with something to learn and try out every week. The TES online community (www.tespro.com)

also offers a huge platform for sharing resources, lesson plans, research and discussion.

At the end of the year, write your own self-evaluation document. Start by doing what the teachers at Clevedon School in Bristol do – ask all the learners to feed back to you on your teaching. They use sticky notes and have a board labelled 'Keep, Change, Grow' where students place their comments under each heading. Of course, they may suggest you change the amount of hard homework – but that will make a great class debate about what will help them achieve the best results. If you listen to such feedback, discuss it with the students and then act on it, imagine how well you will be demonstrating to them that you are a learner for life too – willing to take critical feedback and grow what is working well and change what isn't. And how much better it is to know what they think rather than carry on in ignorance? (See Chapter 4 for more information about self-coaching.)

The very best teachers have a suggestions board or box that sustains a continuous dialogue with pupils about what they are learning and how they are learning it. Other teachers run a weekly class feedback forum or build time to reflect on how learning has happened into their lessons, asking questions such as: What skills and content did you learn from the teacher? How much from your peers? How much from the internet?

A pupils' learning log like this provides an invaluable and informative tool for teachers to browse through, and it has the added bonus that it nurtures a language for learning in your pupils that becomes second nature. It develops their ability to think about learning and how it works. This process of metacognition gets you and your learners to step back from the chalkface and consider what is working and why – so that you can both make it work better and better over time.

> If it's working, stick with it, if it isn't – change it – especially if your pupils tell you so!

In *Visible Learning for Teachers*, Hattie suggests that teachers ask themselves a series of self-evaluation questions addressing issues such as whether your current strategies are working, comparing the merits of different techniques, drilling down into the effectiveness of your methods on learning, and interrogating whether your conception of progress is the same as your colleagues'.[9] This will need to be part of your own (self) performance management as, with the new arrangements for performance-related pay, it really is in your interest to reflect and gather evidence of your impact. Then, if it is not working, you can show how you are responding through planning alternative strategies.

---

9   Hattie, *Visible Learning for Teachers*, p. 161.

Top tips

Evaluate your everyday practice in a non-judgemental way by asking: 'What did I learn from that?' and 'What amendments can I make to get a better result?'

Soak up all the feedback you can get. If it is critical, try consciously to not blame yourself or others – just decide what you are going to do about it.

Take advantage of every lesson observation (from leaders, inspectors or students) as an opportunity to learn. Request feedback, make notes and learn from it.

Take time out to reflect on how you are thinking and feeling on a regular basis and remind yourself that you have a choice about how you feel.

Practise the process of metacognition. Think about, then get control over your moods using meditation, mindfulness, exercise and challenging your mood when you are feeling negative.

Mentally rehearse your next lesson going well – during this, remind yourself of your core principles and beliefs about why you came into this profession.

Mindset 2: Believe you can make a difference

'I know what I do in the classroom can make a big impact on a child's potential – no matter what their starting point ...'

> Teachers/leaders believe that success and failure in student learning is about what they, as teachers or leaders, did or did not do ... We are change agents!
>
> John Hattie[10]

The most important thing you can do to be an outstanding teacher is to realise and believe that you *can* make a difference. A teacher's belief about how much he or she can influence outcomes has the greatest impact on students. (This doesn't, however, absolve the pupils from their contribution and responsibility!)

Do you believe the following statements?

- High expectations are essential and that children can always achieve more than we think.
- It is important to teach varied learning strategies to all pupils so that they can access their learning potential.
- Students who understand progression levels will make more progress because they are more capable of self-assessment and self-adjustment.

---

10 Hattie, *Visible Learning for Teachers*, p. 161.

▨ Peer learning and peer teaching are powerful for learning.

▨ Making mistakes and being able to take critical feedback are crucial for improving learning.

▨ The challenges presented by poverty, parenting, ethnic background, social class and home resources are surmountable.

What you believe as a teacher, especially in the current climate of expectation and accountability, is influenced and reinforced by your training and the culture of the school. But your core values, and the reasons you became a teacher, will help motivate and inspire you to become the best teacher you can be. According to Hattie, the conviction that you are a 'change agent', that you can make a difference because you believe that the outcomes for all children are not fixed, but influenced by us, is crucial to successful teaching.[11] He quotes from Alfieri and colleagues' 2011 article in confirming research findings that teachers need to direct discovery through 'feedback, worked examples, scaffolding and elicited explanation' as activators of learning.[12] This places a high emphasis on the moral aspects of teaching. The best teachers have a mission, and that mission drives their practice to intervene with their pupils to help them become great learners.

---

11 Hattie, *Visible Learning for Teachers*, p. 162.
12 L. Alfieri, P. J. Brooks, N. J. Aldrich and H. R. Tenenbaum, 'Does Discovery-Based Instruction Enhance Learning?' *Journal of Educational Psychology* 103(1) (2011): 1–18, at 12.

Most teachers believe that passing exams is important, but that using the skills and knowledge gained at school to become a successful human being and citizen is the greater goal of education. The teacher who believes that this is the job they are meant to do, helping every child learn and make progress without limits, will be building the bedrock of 'perfect' teaching.

> Teachers need to see themselves as instigators of a change process that can happen in any child's brain. Neuroscientists now tell us that children are 'building their brain' when they are in school and the purpose of education is to grow intelligence. When you educate someone, you are changing their brain. That is what education is for.
>
> Paul Howard-Jones[13]

Mindset 3: Learning to be curious about learning

Be endlessly curious about learning: Why did/didn't that work today? What is it that will make that child make a breakthrough?

The third mindset is about having an endless fascination with learning – how it works and why it works (or doesn't). For learners who struggle, the worst thing that can happen in their schooling is that teachers keep doing the same things in the same unsuccessful way, over and over again – and

---

13 Paul Howard-Jones, *Times Educational Supplement*, 1 March 2013.

expect a different result. Schools that constantly reflect on what works, and doesn't work, in the classroom create a mindset of enquiry that means they are always learning about learning.

> The best schools obsess about improving teaching.
>
> Susan Gregory[14]

The best teachers need to be endlessly flexible in their approaches to teaching and assessment, attending closely to feedback and responses so that they can continually adjust and amend their plans so that each child can make good progress.

> In Year 9, some bottom-set English classes are learning to improve their literacy and communication skills in the same way that they were learning to do so in Year 4 – and Years 5, 6, 7 and 8 ... No wonder they are turned off school, believe they're stupid and are bored out of their heads!
>
> English teacher

14 Susan Gregory, National Director Education and Early Years Introduces the Schools Report 2011/12 [video transcript] (27 November 2012). Available at: http://www.ofsted.gov.uk/resources/ofsted-annual-report-201112-susan-gregory-national-director-education-and-early-years-introduces-sch (accessed 27 September 2013).

According to Hattie, being interested in learning means that teachers need to be: 'adaptive learning experts, to know multiple ways of teaching and learning to be able to coach and model different ways of learning, and to be the best error detectors in the business'.[15] To become a 'learning expert', you need to obsess about learning – and you have the perfect opportunity to do that every day as you observe your pupils growing their brains, adapting their skills, making connections and deepening their learning under your guidance. Develop a mindset that never stops puzzling over what works best and why.

Top tips

In your learning log, list things you would like to try, new words, comments you overhear from children or inspirational words you can share.

Every day, try something new and note what you learn from it. Notice how you learn new skills and unlearn old ones. Become aware of when you go into automatic pilot and stop focusing on the details that make your teaching work brilliantly.

Carry out some informal action research, maybe on an individual pupil or a class activity. Keep a note in your learning log, share it on Twitter, on your blog or deliver

---

15 Hattie, *Visible Learning for Teachers*, p. 163.

an INSET on the outcomes. Start a debate to extend the enquiry.

Talk formally and informally to your classes to get feedback about your lessons. Look for trends and gather ideas for developing your teaching techniques.

Visit other classrooms as often as possible and note anything positive, negative or interesting in your learning log.

Engage in dialogue, not monologue, with your pupils so that you give them a chance to develop their thinking around the topic and give you a chance to actively listen to how their learning is developing.

Mindset 4:
Know that feedback is the breakfast of champions

'I really prioritise giving and getting great feedback to grow my skills and help my pupils make more progress'

Assessment provides feedback for improving teaching and feedback is the crucial nourishment for growth. When you assess progress, this is also giving you the knowledge you need to become a better teacher: Have they got it or not? Did they learn what I thought they did, or more, or less? How can I now assess it and really know they have learnt it?

This mindset is about realising that assessment is not only about assessing the pupils' progress – it is actually about assessing our own impact. The best teachers accept that results are a reflection of their teaching ability – even when the class is lazy or naughty. We want pupils to take responsibility for their own progress and outcomes, but the tricky thing is that developing that independence and self-motivation is *our* responsibility. We know that the home background and parenting of pupils will make this job harder or easier but, in the time that they are with us, we need to teach them how to be great learners. We can do this by providing very regular written and oral feedback that helps them understand how they are doing and how they can do better. Then making sure they act on our advice.

Feedback is powerful for learning. Research by the Sutton Trust found that feedback made the most difference in closing the gap for disadvantaged children.[16] So, how can we make it work for us in the classroom?

Top tips

Be clear about goals and success criteria.

Help pupils constantly adjust by coaching and prompting them to assess their progress against those goals.

---

16 S. Higgins, D. Kokotsaki and R. J. Coe, *Toolkit of Strategies to Improve Learning: Summary for Schools Spending the Pupil Premium* (London: Sutton Trust, 2011).

Rename 'marking' as 'feedback' and make its purpose to help you know how pupils are progressing and actively help them improve (see Chapter 4).

Use questions to promote thinking, such as 'What could you do next to help you move on?', 'How could this be even better?' and 'Is there any way you would do this differently next time?'

Use a variety of tests, quizzes, assessments and other progress checks, and reward effort and response to feedback.

Ensure the pupils are trained in peer assessment techniques against clear assessment criteria.

Give opportunities for accurate, guided self-assessment so you encourage the same metacognitive habits that work for you.

Mindset 5: Expect more of pupils

'I know that my pupils can always achieve more than I think they can'

Constant changes in government policy, school systems, the national curriculum and examinations means teaching has never been more challenging. In addition, in the digital age, learning through social media presents a whole new set of dynamic challenges.

Adapting to change and challenge is not optional but essential to ensure you can be a great teacher in the 21st century. When you have a mindset that loves change, challenge and risk, you are open to the possibility that the children might know more than you and can enjoy teaching you how to podcast, Skype or use their phone and tablet apps. The other crucial aspect of this mindset is that you honestly believe that children are capable of so much more than we ever could have imagined:

- They know more than we think they do.
- They can achieve more than their targets suggest.
- They will constantly surprise us with their sensitivity and maturity when we give them added responsibility.

Entering a classroom and expecting to be surprised by how much your pupils will achieve means you will always have the highest expectations and will communicate this to them. This may seem idealistic – of course, some children will find things hard. But in the same way that a healthy baby never considers the possibility of failing to learn to walk or talk – no matter how long it takes and how many times they fall over – a great teacher doesn't see failure as an option. If it doesn't work then you try another way, and if that doesn't work you try another way, and if that doesn't work you try another way and so on – until it works.

Pupils who catch this mindset from their teachers believe that the learning never ends. Teachers who do their best but think they know the limitations of their students are destined to settle for mediocrity.

> The art of teaching is the 'constant attention to individual differences' not so that it can be broken down into bite-size pieces that make it easy to pass exams but so that the students are engaged themselves in 'the challenge of the learning'.
>
> John Hattie[17]

This challenge – to believe anything is possible – is huge and scary for both teachers and pupils. Pupils need to know that learning can be hard, can be painful, risks failure (and that this is part of the process) and can be boring, repetitive and frustrating, as well as fun and fascinating. The very best teachers share this with their pupils and know how to get them into the challenging terrain outside of their comfort zones with the help of unconditional support from their peers. As pupils grow into those zones, they learn that through taking risks they can do more and the learning becomes less scary.

Risk-taking is essential for learners if they are going to make maximum progress. Trying harder activities, reading difficult texts, solving 'impossible' problems and learning to play that complex piece are the types of challenge that make pupils

---

17 Hattie, *Visible Learning for Teachers*, p. 164.

start to get the habits of persistence and resilience they need to be successful.

> A job isn't worth doing if it isn't scary.
>
> Jasmine Whitbread[18]

Making homework a highly effective learning experience is a constant challenge for the 'perfect' teacher to tackle. The very best teachers will set challenging work that extends learning beyond the lesson and isn't just a bolt-on to please parents. Motivating pupils to enjoy 'home learning' by applying their schoolwork in extended projects to life outside or 'flipping classrooms' (see Chapter 4), so that they learn at home and then use that learning in lessons, may offer great opportunities to challenge your class.

Top tips

Suspend any disbelief so that anything is possible and approach every lesson expecting the best.

Believe that all pupils have the resources to make good progress – we just need to find the right strategy.

---

18 Jasmine Whitbread, CEO of Save the Children, *Woman's Hour*, BBC Radio 4, 31 July 2013.

Don't get mad, get curious. If learning doesn't go well, don't blame yourself or the kids – just adapt what you are doing until it works better.

Encourage the pupils to have high expectations of themselves by establishing a culture that understands that learning requires hard work and that if they aren't feeling challenged, then they aren't growing their brains.

Set homework that is motivating, extends learning and makes it connect with the lives of your pupils.

Mindset 6: Collaborate to grow

'I always take regular opportunities to work with colleagues outside my subject/phase and I always learn something new from it'

Believe in the power of collaboration from teacher to teacher and pupil to pupil; when we work together we make more progress. There is a synergy in interdependency which will enable you to connect with other people and help you always to do better together.

If you adopt this as a principle in your working life, you will share ideas, resources, problems and strategies in such a powerful way that it will maximise your impact as a teacher. Not only that, but you will improve your own communication skills to become a better networker and be more popular, charismatic and influential!

What happens when you help someone else to improve? Do you benefit when you generously give your time and energy to support someone else in their learning journey and it works? Have you learned anything from helping another teacher or colleague overcome a challenge?

Apart from the feel-good factor, there is good evidence that collaboration and peer learning actually embeds our own learning more effectively than anything else. So when we teach, we learn. When children teach each other, they deepen their understanding and secure their knowledge and concepts.

Does your class know how powerful collaboration is? Do you train them to communicate effectively so that they can make the most of working in groups and teams? Taking on various team roles, giving and receiving feedback, discussing, debating and negotiating solutions to problems are all activities that will build those essential collaborative skills.

Imagine if, in your classroom, every pupil gave unconditional support to others to help them make the maximum progress. Pupils would be unafraid to ask and answer questions, would take more risks and would improve their progress. Teachers who believe it is a major part of their role to develop positive relationships in classrooms and staffrooms know that those who 'fire together, wire together', and thereby create powerful learning communities.

Top tips

Work with your colleagues to plan, teach and assess together as often as possible.

Habitually share resources, ideas and strategies with other colleagues.

Get involved in working parties, training events and extra-curricular days as often as possible.

In your classes and department, establish zero tolerance of put-downs and big rewards for unconditional support for each other's learning and progress.

Value collaborative learning in your classroom.

Encourage talking, planning and thinking in structured and unstructured ways.

Improve communication skills by encouraging opportunities for public speaking, debating and teaching each other.

Mindset 7: Use a language of learning

'We talk about learning with pupils and parents so they can understand how to help create new learning strategies and solutions'

The best teachers say: 'I am passionate about and promote the language of learning'.[19] Learning is a process that happens invisibly inside our heads. Teaching pupils to reflect on what they have learned and, most importantly, how they have learned (or did not and why) starts to make the learning process more visible for them.

> Many professions have a language that defines their activity and encourages debate and discussion about strategies. Giving teachers and parents a language to help them talk to their children about their learning has led to enhanced engagement by students in their schooling experiences.
>
> John Hattie[20]

Which words describe learning for you and your pupils? Thinking, creating, remembering, considering, imagining, deciding, choosing, hypothesising, rehearsing, studying, swotting, absorbing, understanding, drafting, practising, listening, speaking, connecting, practising, reading, writing, questioning, seeing, hearing, feeling, tasting, touching ...

This reflective process can help pupils to take more ownership and responsibility for their learning and so become more self-managing and self-aware. When parents can also take part in

19 Hattie, *Visible Learning for Teachers*, p. 5.
20 Hattie, *Visible Learning for Teachers*, p. 165.

these discussions, after school and in the holidays, their contribution can only improve great learning habits.

This requires a language for learning that gives pupils a vocabulary they can use to discuss and debate the process of learning and communicate how it works for them.

At a recent CPD event, Dylan Wiliam suggested that children from more educated/affluent backgrounds often know the 'rules' of the classroom and the language of learning before they come to school and consequently are better learners from the outset.

He illustrated this jokingly by saying that you can tell the class of a family by the questions they ask their child in a supermarket. Middle class parents tend to ask questions like: 'Which is the best price/value?' A lower class parent would ask 'Do you want a smack?'

Regularly using a language for learning and sharing the success criteria for progress will help learners understand exactly what they need to do to improve, help them to discuss and track their progress and help them to address their weaknesses with more confidence and courage. Ofsted inspectors are looking for pupils who understand how to improve their work and have high levels of engagement and commitment to learning, alongside resilience and independence.

> Outstanding teachers 'ensure students are engaged in learning, and generate high levels of commitment to learning across the school'.
>
> Ofsted, *School Inspection Handbook* (2013): 39

When teachers nurture a language for learning in their classrooms, it develops students who are more self-motivated, who can debate their progress and who can take feedback and constructive criticism maturely. Being able to dispassionately evaluate our own and each other's work against success criteria makes us better able to take criticism because we know it will help us to move forward and make progress in our learning.

If students are able to talk about a variety of learning strategies, they are usually better at spotting mistakes and see them as an opportunity to learn – not as a symptom of failure. A language for learning makes it easier for students to understand that learned helplessness and dependency are the result if they are towed through tests by the teacher. They will also learn that resilience and the ability to learn by yourself, for yourself, will deliver lifelong learning skills.[21]

---

21 Kate Wall, Elaine Hall, Vivienne Baumfield, et al., *Learning to Learn in School Phase 4 and Learning to Learn in Further Education* (London: Campaign for Learning, 2010). Available at: http://www.campaign-for-learning.org.uk/cfl/learninginschools/projects/learningtolearn/news/casestudies/index.asp (accessed 11 September 2013).

Features of a growth-mindset language for learning

- There is a change from a 'judge and be judged' to a 'learn and help learn' mindset.
- Pupils use language such as: effort, goals, practice, coach, support, feedback, develop, create, collaborate, resilience, learn, grow, challenge, connections, reflect, review, consider and communicate.
- Pupils will be able to respond eloquently to questions such as: 'How did a mistake or setback teach you something today?'

Language makes our learning 'visible'

When John Hattie talks about 'visible learning' inside a school, he shows how making learning processes clear and evident for all our students helps them to make better progress and become more successful and self-motivated learners. He provides clear evidence that the formula for successful schooling involves teachers becoming more aware of their impact and also that the more 'the student becomes the teacher and the more the teacher becomes the learner, then the more successful are the outcomes'.[22] This requires a shared language for learning.

---

22 Hattie, *Visible Learning for Teachers*, p. 17.

Subject progress

Teachers that instil a love of their subject in learners and a desire to know more are the teachers we remember. Children mirror these teachers' enthusiasm and passion and tackle the challenges of learning with more resilience and enthusiasm. Hattie notes how important this is:

> Passion reflects the thrill, as well as the frustrations, of learning, it can be infectious, it can be taught, it can be modelled, and it can be learnt.[23]

Beyond a passionate delivery however Ofsted inspectors will be looking for progress in your lessons. You need to prepare your students so that when inspectors have conversations with individual students they can express:

- What they are learning in your lessons and why.
- How they are learning.
- How it links to other areas of learning.
- What they need to do next.

Students who are used to metacognition, and who have the language needed to express their reflections on learning, will be able to articulate the learning intentions of your lesson in their own words and comment on the wider context and purpose of the lesson, as the example below illustrates.

---

23 Hattie, *Visible Learning for Teachers*, p. 16.

Ofsted inspector: Why are you learning about volcanoes?

Answer 1: Don't know really. I suppose it's because we have to do it in science.

Answer 2: Because they're important in forming new rocks, are dangerous for people living near them and put lots of CO_2 into the air. This means they're linked to the stuff we did about global climate and to what we did about plate tectonics and to the stuff we did about human geography and the earth's history, and extinctions ... Want to know how?

How a student answers a question can tell us so much about the way they have been taught.

The continuum model

Ensure that you (and your pupils) are very clear about the progression model in your subject. Use differentiated objectives to clarify how the learning journey could progress. David Didau, author of *The Perfect English Lesson*,[24] developed the continuum model – from my *The Perfect Ofsted Lesson*[25] – so his students could understand their starting points and where they needed to go. To encourage a growth mindset, the continuum represents the learning journey and how the learning

---

24 D. Didau, *The Perfect Ofsted English Lesson* (Carmarthen: Independent Thinking Press, 2012).
25 J. Beere, *The Perfect Ofsted Lesson* (Carmarthen: Crown House Publishing, 2012).

deepens as we learn enough to *apply* our ideas. The table below provides an example of this.

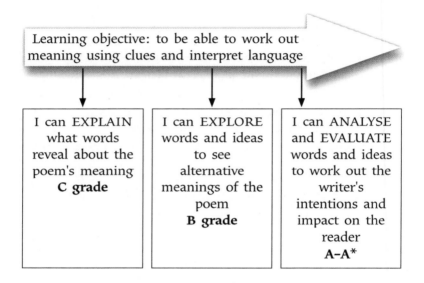

I can EXPLAIN what words reveal about the poem's meaning
C grade

I can EXPLORE words and ideas to see alternative meanings of the poem
B grade

I can ANALYSE and EVALUATE words and ideas to work out the writer's intentions and impact on the reader
A–A*

Teach them to be curious about learning

When students can talk about the way they learn, it helps them to take more control and responsibility for their own progress. Many well-educated parents with the money and know-how spend lots of time talking to their children from the time they are born. They run a descriptive narrative of the world around their growing child which allows these children to accumulate more than twice as many words in their vocabulary by the time they arrive in reception class as their peers. They have had their why, what, when and how questions answered – so they want to keep asking and wondering and thinking and learning. By the age of 7, the destiny of many these pupils has been substantially programmed by their ability to have a dialogue about the things they learn. Some will not have benefitted from a family life that promotes debate and discussion about their learning in school. An excellent teacher will work hard with such children to develop this language for learning to help them close the gap in achievement – which will continue to widen unless they can talk and think about how they learn.

Deliberately develop a language for learning with your underachievers

Your impact as a teacher will be judged by how your pupils achieve and, in particular, by how you help those who are not making enough progress to improve their outcomes. When your school is inspected, work will be scrutinised and inspectors will speak with pupils about their learning. Inspectors will particularly track and talk to pupils who have extra needs, or who haven't made enough progress, to see how they are being supported across different lessons to make the necessary progress. If your pupils are used to talking about their learning, and have a vocabulary to describe it, they will be able to explain how they are making progress very accurately for anyone who cares to ask. However, without knowing how to talk and think about learning and how it works, your vulnerable learners could always be behind the starting line in lessons.

Top tips

Engage the pupils in the learning intentions/outcomes/ objectives – whatever you call them.

Make sure they know the wider context of the learning and its relevance to their everyday lives.

Talk about the 'how' of learning as well as the 'what' in every lesson – involve them in the process and planning.

Give your pupils useful vocabulary to describe both their subject-based and skills-based learning experiences – check they aren't just echoing back to you, but really get it.

Encourage peer assessment and peer feedback that uses language of learning.

Get the pupils to design posters about learning to display in classrooms.

Lay down a philosophy for developing the habits of great learning that includes words such as optimism, empathy, support, resilience, determination, curiosity, creativity, collaboration and enquiry.

Give pupils rewards for demonstrating these qualities and reinforce them by recognising and commenting on them.

Run a learning to learn programme for your support staff and pupils and encourage them to research how learning works for them.

Complete the growth mindset health check (see Appendix 1) to help you put these mindsets into practice every day.

Why I still love teaching

As a shiny NQT in the late 1970s, my enthusiasm knew no bounds. I was excited about the prospect of passing on my own passion for English, but even more importantly, encouraging them to develop a lifelong curiosity for learning that would see them fulfil their own dreams and ambitions. Looking back, after 36 years in the profession, such romantic sentiments might seem outdated, but they are still the stepping-stones that ensure that I have maintained my enjoyment and creative impetus that are probably the raison d'être of a long career.

The support and advice of two much-admired English advisors in these early days, Bill Shaw and Charles Byrne, is still highly relevant to me today. The first gem was the need to become a facilitator, rather than 'just a teacher', so that my charges could evolve into independent learners. To this end, I use the Socratic dialogue technique to develop high-level oral skills, regular improvisation and a well-stocked props cupboard to stimulate the imaginative and risk-taking behaviours that make learning fun. Also, small-group projects seem to enable students of all abilities and characters to think more laterally.

A second nugget of advice was to nurture quality teacher–pupil relationships that will ensure cooperation in any scenario. My own experience of this includes a consistent daily routine. For my subject, this includes student-reading at the start of a lesson, so that I can present the objectives, deal with any extraneous issues and talk to them on a more personal level to establish rapport. I love to engender a sense of fun through the use of drama, telling jokes, sharing quotes or quips and a weekly challenge. I always invest time outside the classroom to share ways of improving work or creative writing that students can produce in their own time.

Finally, a third suggestion by my earliest gurus was to take the creation of lesson ambience very seriously indeed. I devise displays and think carefully about furniture layout. Ambience is far more than this, however, to me, it signifies the imparting of high expectations regarding behaviour, oral and written responses and general attitudes. It starts from a friendly greeting at the door; it reflects fairness, humour, kindness and praise from me as practitioner, but also between the pupils themselves; and it is respectful about the fear they often feel at school and seeks to put them at ease. For example, I instigated sixth-form breakfasts as part of our lesson to help new classes gel together.

Above all else, teaching, for me, is the engendering of a sense of wonder and belief that anyone can make incredible progress – including myself.

Why do I still love teaching? I would hope that a sense of a learning adventure remains my lasting legacy. A student's awe at learning something new is the key, in my humble opinion, to a lifetime of happy and successful teaching.

Carole Lewis, English teacher

Chapter 2
Creating rapport for learning

> *I've never forgotten those English lessons – we had such a great time and worked so hard that I got my only A. Everything I know about the English language I learned from you!*

This was said by someone I taught 20 years ago when I bumped into her at a training event very recently. I also remembered her class with huge affection because it was my first A level class. I had no English degree – I was learning with them and staying just one step ahead – yet they all overachieved on their target grades. And we had the very best time together. So why did it work?

To create rapport, begin with the outcome in mind: you want your classes to fulfil their potential, work hard and love their lessons. Teaching is not just for exams and qualifications – it is life-changing, character-building, society-making stuff that happens every day for five hours a day, five days a week, 38 weeks a year, for 13-plus years. That's 12,350 hours of opportunity to help young people live better and more successful lives – whatever their starting points. It is why teachers matter so much more than policies or politics.

Nothing is more important than the relationships you build up with your classes because they will respond to your lessons emotionally before they learn the 3Rs and all the other content. Don't underestimate the effect you have on your pupils' mirror neurons – the brain cells that respond to other people's moods and develop empathy. Critical links between emotions and the cognitive patterning needed for learning are now well established.[1] As Andrew Curran so succinctly describes it in his *Little Book of Big Stuff about the Brain*, 'all it takes is love':

> [T]he most surprising message for me, looking through millions of dollars of research, is that the most important thing you can do for yourself and others is to love yourself and others for who they are because by doing that you maximise the brain's ability to learn and unlearn.[2]

Building relationships between you and your class, and between the pupils within your class, couldn't be more impor-

---

1   See, for example, E. Jensen, *The Learning Brain* (San Diego, CA: Turning Point, 1995), p. 38.
2   Curran, *The Little Book of Big Stuff about the Brain*, p. 1.

tant for them to make maximum progress. Daniel Ebb argues that you learn things because your nerve cells join together and that makes them fire together: 'nerve cells that fire together, wire together' and this is 'predominantly under the control of your emotional system'.[3] The more emotion there is in a situation, the more likely it is you will learn from it. So, engaging your pupils means engaging their emotional brains, because this way your teaching will stay with them and inspire them beyond their school experience.

> Which teachers do you remember from your own schooling and why?
>
> What do you want your pupils to say about you in ten years' time?
>
> How many of your pupils have you helped become better learners for life?

First, give them what every human being requires – a feeling of being valued and understood. This doesn't mean being cuddly and sweet, with everyone being nice to each other and the teacher praising ten times for every criticism. It means believing that the children in your class can and will learn and make progress – and conveying that to them with relentless enthusiasm and love. It means having the very highest expectations of their behaviour and potential and being ruthlessly consistent in demanding the best of both, remembering

---

3 Quoted in Curran, *The Little Book of Big stuff about the Brain*, p. 26.

that every word and action sends a message. It means that, as teachers, we must nurture a growth mindset in our pupils (see Chapter 1).

Mindset tweak

Believing that every child has the potential to succeed – if only we can find the right way – is the principle that will help you make the most difference.

Carol Dweck examines great teachers in her book, *Mindset: The Psychology of Success.* She tells the story of Marva Collins who taught children in Chicago who had been judged and discarded by the system. The children in her classes were extreme: one boy would slash his classmates' clothing with blades he removed from pencil sharpeners; another, who had been rejected by a mental health centre, stabbed children with pencils; others had been excluded multiple times, one from 13 schools; one hit another student with a hammer; another threatened suicide in almost every sentence. Collins was their last hope. She told them:

I know most of you can't spell your name. You don't know the alphabet, you don't know how to read, you don't know homonyms or how to syllabicate. I promise you that you will. None of you has ever failed. School may have failed you. Well goodbye to failure, children.

> Welcome to success. You will read hard books in here and understand what you read. You will write every day ... But you must help me to help you. If you don't give anything don't expect anything.[4]

The progress of her students was rapid. Their response to the tough love and learning regime? 'We do hard things here. They fill your brain' was the observation of one student when quizzed about the school.

Dweck studied other teachers who had achieved rapid progress and outstanding outcomes with all ability levels, and discovered that high expectations (sometimes ridiculously so) and the thrill of seeing children grow in terms of skills and expertise were the ingredients that made such teachers immensely curious about how to help them make progress.

Marva Collins set extremely high standards, right from the start. She introduced words and concepts that were, at first, way above what her students could grasp. Yet, from day one she established an atmosphere of genuine affection and concern as she promised students they would succeed. She said to the boy who wouldn't try: 'I'm gonna love you ... I love you already and I'm gonna love you even when you don't love yourself.'[5]

---

4   Dweck, *Mindset*, p. 194.
5   Dweck, *Mindset*, p. 196.

This type of 'challenge and nurture' approach – caring about every pupil regardless of previous achievement but with an unflinching determination to ensure they learn and make progress – is needed in every classroom. With Marva Collins, this led to 7-year-olds reading the *Wall Street Journal*, older children discussing Plato's *Republic* and a reading list that included the complete works of Anton Chekhov, *The Canterbury Tales* and Bamberger's *Physics through Experiment*.

Getting in 'flow' with your class

Gaining rapport with your classes creates a synergy that means you can challenge learners to achieve way beyond their own expectations. You will get that 'flow' experience in your class when you have connected with their world enough to gain true rapport and when you are all 'firing together'. This means working towards the same goals and loving the experience. The very best feeling you can have as a teacher is when you and your class are in flow. So, how do you achieve this? The strategies used in neuro-linguistic programming (NLP) have provided the most powerful tools I have found for understanding how to create great rapport (see below for more on this).

Use body language, sensitive questioning and flexible approaches to help you tune in to your students' world. This means observing intently the mood of individuals and the class and responding accordingly. It means mirroring an individual's body language a little and chatting to them about how their football team got on at the weekend. It means taking an interest in the music they like and knowing a bit about the television programmes and social media they love so that you can relate authentically with them.

> Outstanding behaviour: 'Pupils' pride in the school is shown by their excellent conduct, manners and punctuality.'
>
> Ofsted, *School Inspection Handbook* (2013): 43

Top tips for behaviour management

Reflect on how you develop your relationships with your classes using this grow–keep–change model for behaviour management:

Grow
A growth mindset that sees learning as a journey Habits of risk-taking, optimism, resilience, empathy, curiosity in pupils and you Link the learning with the real world they live in Consequences for actions – good and bad A belief that anything is possible – if we can find a way

Keep
Consistent boundaries
Constructive criticism
Challenging work that is hard enough to grow their brains
Feedback that makes them think in new ways and find new solutions
Relationships that value each individual child
Rewards for effort, not just outcomes
Enthusiasm for the subject
Focus on progress

Change
Praise that isn't deserved
Strategies that don't work
Empty threats you can't follow up
Feedback that thinks for them
Feedback that is descriptive and vague
Taking it personally when they say f*** off
Giving up on them when they give up on themselves

Many of the very best strategies for developing good rapport and great relationships with learners come from the field of NLP, which is a study of communication and its impact on our thinking and our performance.

NLP and managing behaviour

The theory and practice of NLP provides a set of principles, techniques and strategies which are applicable to all aspects of your teaching (and personal) life. NLP is the study of excellence and of the 'software' of the mind that creates excellence. There is a huge amount of theory and jargon around this subject, but this section simply aims to summarise those aspects of NLP which have been found to be the most useful for teaching and learning in a classroom.

Four Durham schools took part in a pilot project in 2006 designed to explore successful interventions that developed high levels of rapport, based on the NLP techniques of Bandler and Grinder.[6] Staff and children seemed to benefit from understanding how to focus on outcomes to achieve better results and communicate in ways that influence thinking.

NLP is about acquiring an attitude – a way of being – that underpins social and emotional intelligence. Its principles enable you to take control of your emotions and respond to others in ways that help you develop perfect rapport – and have a really powerful impact in the classroom. It has helped me in my personal as well as my professional life. In fact, it has become part of me, giving me the skills to 'think on purpose' (metacognition) and develop the confidence to learn to become a highly effective teacher, school leader and trainer.

---

6   R. Churches and R. Terry, *NLP for Teachers: How to Be a Highly Effective Teacher* (Carmarthen: Crown House Publishing, 2007).

> At best, IQ contributes about 20 percent to the factors that determine life success, which leaves 80 percent to other forces [like] emotional intelligence: abilities such as being able to motivate oneself and persist in the face of frustrations; to control impulse and delay gratification; to regulate one's moods and keep distress from swamping the ability to think; to empathize and to hope.
>
> Daniel Goleman[7]

Put simply, NLP looks at the way successful people think and suggests how you can think like that too. Imagine what might happen if you followed the five principles below and measured all your activities against them when reflecting on your performance (you will notice lots of overlap with the mindsets in Chapter 1 and habits in Chapter 4)?

1. Focus on the outcome you want

Do you know exactly what it is you want to achieve and what it looks like?

NLP is relentlessly focused on outcomes – really congruent outcomes. In other words, outcomes you totally believe in and know you can make happen. This means that all you say and do is passionately channelled towards them. They are not objectives simply written on the board.

---

7   D. Goleman, *Emotional Intelligence: Why It Matters More Than IQ* (London: Bloomsbury, 1996), p. 34.

The secret to achieving the outcomes is flexibility. If you are not succeeding, try something else, and if that doesn't work then try something else and so on. (One definition of madness is to keep doing the same thing again and again but expecting a different result!) The teachers who make the most powerful impact on socially deprived low achievers are those who focus on highly ambitious goals for these students and work tirelessly towards them – no matter what the obstacles, as seen in Carol Dweck's research described above.

How does it work in the classroom?

In assessment for learning strategies:

- Set clear, engaging short-term objectives. Help students work out the success criteria and review them at the end to measure progress.
- Set long-term goals (with success criteria) that students believe in and which are used as coaching tools.
- Set yourself short- and long-term goals, again with success criteria.

2. **There's no such thing as failure – only feedback**

Imagine if students in your classroom really believed that they couldn't fail because *every* part of the learning process – even failure – was part of the journey towards success. Imagine if they *really* listened to advice and constructive criticism and they all supported each other's learning unconditionally, so that the only peer pressure was aimed at achieving the very best. Imagine if you, as a teacher, *truly* believed that every mistake was a learning experience and that improvement comes if you (and your students) are constantly open to advice and willing to adapt your methods.

The very best learners are curious about learning and are willing to relentlessly seek out all possibilities for improving – no matter how many knockbacks, wrong turns, rewrites or disappointments there are. If you can model this mindset to the children, you will help them (and you) master the secret of resilience in learning.

How does it work in the classroom?

● Have Dedicated Improvement and Reflection Time (DIRT) in the lesson.[8] This is properly trained peer assessment or self-assessment where students measure their progress against the original objectives in mini plenaries and think about how they have learned – what worked and what didn't. They spend time on improving their work, amending it and responding to feedback.

● Redefine marking as feedback.

● Demand a response to feedback – get pupils to act on your feedback and say what they are going to do next.

● Model every mistake as a learning experience. Encourage pupils to correct your spellings or teach you how to download an app, or let them give you

---

8   See Beere, *The Perfect Ofsted Lesson*, p. 29.

feedback about your teaching (see also Principle 3 below).

● Deliver discrete lessons in resilience and mood control that help students to practise the habit of deferring gratification, developing optimism and creating aspirational goals.[9]

3. The meaning of your communication is the response you get

If you are misunderstood and get a different outcome from what you wanted, it is up to you to change how you communicate to get the desired outcome. This is a very powerful principle because it means *you* take the responsibility for the outcomes of what you say and do. Taking this responsibility will change your life! If someone is being impossible and reacting differently to how you had hoped, try communicating in another way until you get the response you want.

Linked to this is the belief that every behaviour has a positive intention. This is sometimes a very hard principle to apply because some behaviour is wrong by all measures, but when you act as if this is true, it is amazingly liberating. Think of the student who seems to hate you, or the member of your team who just won't get reports in on time, or the neighbour who is rude and upsets you. First, recognise that they are behaving in this way for their own survival and they may not be able to change. Second,

---

9   For a programme of lessons, see Jackie Beere's *The Learner's Toolkit* (Carmarthen: Crown House Publishing, 2007) and *The Primary Learner's Toolkit* (Carmarthen: Crown House Publishing, 2010).

think how *you* can change your responses to their behaviour. Can you change what you do or say – or how you do or say it – to get the outcome you had hoped for? Focus on the outcome you want, rather than on fairness or justice or revenge. Anything is possible if you can get rapport by understanding the other person's emotional state and connecting in a positive way.

How does it work in the classroom?

- When teaching, focus on the response you are getting and check out if you need to change the communication. If the class look bored, change the pace/activity/topic (see also Mindset 4 in Chapter 1).

- Start seeing yourself as others see you. Get feedback about your performance from your classes, your colleagues and your managers. Ask questions or give out simple questionnaires: What do you enjoy about my lessons? How could I improve learning for you? Do we meet lesson objectives? Do you feel safe and confident in my lessons?

- Allow time in meetings for reflection on how each of you could do one thing differently to help each other.

Some of the feedback you get may not be easy to hear, but if you know about any weak points then you can adapt and improve.

4. **Being a flexible, adaptable communicator who takes full responsibility for responses, gives you the ultimate gift of rapport**

If you have really applied the thinking above, you will find that you have learned to take much more control of your own emotions. Now you can begin to take control of the emotions of others – in a nice way!

You can continually adapt your style, language, body language, register and so on until whoever you are talking to feels amazingly comfortable and at ease. You can make each class feel like they are your favourite class, make everyone in your team feel valued and get your students to be in tune with your passion for the highest standards of achievement.

How does it work in the classroom?

- Mirror and match the mood of your classes.
- Understand their world of technology, music and sport – or whatever turns them on – and use it shamelessly to gain rapport.
- Do so particularly with the disengaged child who sees school as a prison sentence and learning as a punishment.

5. **All experience has structure that we can replicate to create self-fulfilling prophecies**

Understanding this leads to techniques for achieving excellence. Start by asking: How is experience structured in the minds of those who are highly successful? These people structure their experience by habitually using the above principles and so demonstrate outstanding social and emotional intelligence.

We can copy the way successful individuals think, and thereby improve our teaching, learning and leadership, if we practise simple techniques – one of which is visualisation. The way we structure experiences is based on VAK (visual, auditory and kinaesthetic inputs). What we see, hear and feel creates our experiences.

Most of us tend to mentally rehearse everything going badly – from public speaking or the next lesson with your worst class to that meeting with the angry parent. We imagine our exams, interviews or important presentations going wrong and set up habits of anxiety and dread around them. We see, hear and feel failure.

If we want to achieve great results, we can instead visualise our desired experience – thinking about what *that* would look, sound and feel like. When you rehearse an event, your brain believes it is experiencing reality, so mentally rehearsing future events with positive outcomes helps to build a self-fulfilling prophecy. Excellent athletes and other performers have learnt this discipline. We can help students do the same by describing desired, positive outcomes passionately and powerfully so that they feel they have already done it once in their heads!

How does it work in the classroom (to improve your teaching)?

- Visualise a time when you are at your most brilliant as a teacher. See the smile on your face and the energy and passion for your lesson. Feel the adrenalin rush of excitement as you see the faces of the children buzzing with enthusiasm for the learning. Hear the clever answers they are giving you, feel the flow of learning and the community support that you have nurtured in that classroom ...
- Now transfer this way of thinking to your least favourite class.

Case study

I was recently observed teaching a Key Stage 4 class, which began to play up, despite my best efforts with planning and resources. I received an 'inadequate' and will be observed again, with the same group, next month. I worry that I will teach a decent lesson but be marked down again because of behaviour. What can I do?

Good focused classroom observations can highlight problems and provide an opportunity to consider how to put relationships right in your class. Teaching is a game of bluff. We can't control a class without some degree of complicity from the pupils – gained by our enthusiasm, their belief that we care and a consistent, relentless application of behavioural boundaries.

In future lessons:

- Take back control by rearranging the seating and pushing them out of their comfort zones.

- Reinforce the school's discipline policy and get the class to agree that rules are essential for them to learn – e.g. respecting each other's views and work, listening to the teacher and each other, giving each other support to make progress.

- Use the secret student technique. Reward or sanction the class for the behaviour of one student whose name is revealed at the end.

- Make objectives engaging so that they see the point of the lesson and know they can achieve something.

- Introduce choice and collaboration – these are powerful incentives for learning.

- Add the challenge of competition between groups and they will be too engaged to get distracted and play the game of winding you up.

- Link the tasks to something they can relate to – e.g. football, computer games, music, film, animals.

- Involve them in the planning.

- Give them responsibility for their learning by co-designing the tasks, building in choices, setting their own success criteria and writing their own tests or objectives.

- Set differentiated objectives and let them decide what they are aiming for and why.

- Set constant challenges – e.g. challenge them to finish work in a given time scale, increase the amount of work to be completed or the number of solutions to be found.

- Relentlessly follow through on the high expectations you have agreed together.

- Jump on the first miscreant and use sanctions for bad behaviour, including contacting home.

- Have the highest expectations of what they can do and how they will behave.

- Combine this with a sincere and stubborn determination to see them succeed.

- Get them up to the front presenting and to show what they have learnt.

- Praise, praise, praise when they have worked hard.

- Tell them you are being observed.

Finally, mentally rehearse all of this regularly, with you firmly and completely in control, with a calm voice and students responding well. Convince yourself that you love them and have the power, control and influence to help them learn. Act as if you do – and (eventually) you will convince them, yourself and your observer!

Top tips

Have high expectations and clear boundaries.

Have consistency of response with relentless follow-through.

Connect with them through sincere affection and curiosity about how to help them make great progress.

Create a climate for learning through your commitment to them and belief in their ability to learn. Show you will never give up on them.

Establish unconditional support for each other's progress and learning amongst your pupils.

Model every mistake as a learning experience so they see learning as a journey and not a destination.

Laugh with them but always show who is in control.

Behaviour for learning

When I ask teachers what makes an outstanding learner, they all agree that such a child would be focused, risk-taking, curious, resilient, determined, self-motivated, self-regulating, able to make mistakes and bounce back and be empathetic.

However, imagine asking our naughtiest pupils who aren't making enough progress and who need to work harder what *they* think makes an outstanding learner. I've tried it and they say things like: 'I should be quiet', 'I should sit still', 'Do as

I am told', 'Work harder', 'Listen to the teacher', 'Stop talking to my neighbour', 'Write neater', 'Be good' and so on. So, there is the gap between what we know we need to nurture as habits of great learning and what they perceive is the magic formula for more approval.

We all know that it isn't enough to be 'good' in lessons in order to make great progress, so the very best lessons will relentlessly nurture the qualities of resilience, curiosity and self-management and create a culture of unconditional support for each other's learning and progress.

The Ofsted descriptor for outstanding behaviour and safety sets the bar at a high level:

> Pupils consistently display a thirst for knowledge and a love of learning, including in independent, group and whole class work, which have a very strong impact on their progress in lessons.
>
> Ofsted, *School Inspection Handbook* (2013): 43

Nurturing this attitude in your classroom means developing the habits of the very best learners for all your class. Reinforce and reward these habits at every opportunity so that all learners become more curious, risk-taking, self-evaluating and resilient with every lesson you teach.

Planning for success: rigorous consistency

Planning engaging, challenging tasks that relate to the real world outside of school is the best way to ensure great behaviour. You will also need to establish a consistent and relentless classroom ethos that has zero tolerance to any disruption of learning. Be meticulous and monomaniacal about establishing kindness, confidence and a love of learning. The habits of behaviour that you have established will be obvious to any inspector. The most powerful way to do this is to enlist the students themselves to understand why these habits are so important and become aware of how they can develop them in themselves and others.

> Skilled and highly consistent behaviour management by all staff makes a strong contribution to an exceptionally positive climate for learning.
>
> Ofsted, *School Inspection Handbook* (2013): 43

Strategies for involving students in improving behaviour for learning

Giving learners ownership and choice generates more commitment and intrinsic motivation. Get pupils to create their own set of 'brilliant learning' laws that fit in with the school's behaviour policy but which create a 'buy-in' for your particular subject, phase and context. Display them prominently and refer to them often. Also:

- Reward high-quality collaborative work and peer assessment.
- Make 'supporting learning for all' a focus for reward and praise.
- Use football and other team analogies to show how working together makes us all winners.
- Explain that they all make more progress when they support each other.
- Say often 'I'm not going to give up on you' until the reluctant learners finally give in and get on with it.

For more on how to use powerful NLP techniques with your pupils read *Confident Classroom Leadership* by Peter Hook and Andy Vass.[10]

What pupils see as the most important attributes of a good teacher are shown below. It is impossible to show all of these

---

10 P. Hook and A. Vass, *Confident Classroom Leadership* (London: David Fulton, 2000).

all of the time, but challenge yourself to demonstrate as many as you can each lesson:

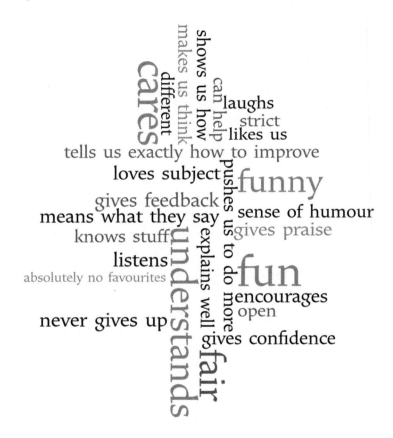

Now that you have wonderful rapport with your classes, you are about to go on an amazing learning journey together. So, what activities and strategies can you use to put all of the thinking in these first two chapters into practice? Read on ...

Chapter 3

Lessons are for learning – what makes the perfect (Ofsted) lesson?

There is no magic formula or tick list for an outstanding lesson. However, there are examples of excellent and interesting practice in this chapter that may suit your particular style. Take these ideas and adapt them to help you deliver great progress for your pupils. The 2013 Ofsted Handbook makes it clear to all school leaders that there are no set rules about how a lesson should be structured:

> Inspectors must not expect teaching staff to teach in any specific way. Schools and teachers should decide for themselves how to teach so that children are engaged in lessons, acquire knowledge and learn well.
>
> Ofsted, *School Inspection Handbook* (2013): 37

A set lesson structure may include an interesting starter, collaborative activity, some peer assessment and a concluding plenary, but may still not work for all the pupils. Some might not make great progress in acquiring knowledge effectively or become fully engaged and challenged to reach their potential. It's not the strategy you use – it's your ability to monitor and evaluate its impact, and adapt accordingly, that will make you the 'perfect' teacher. Whatever way you teach, never stop having that self-evaluating mindset (outlined in Chapter 1), so that you know your impact.

There is much to be said for ringing the changes and varying your style and methods. Keeping pupils on their toes, not quite knowing what to expect, is a powerful way to engage and will create that excited 'What are we doing today, Sir?' thirst for learning.

Growing great learners in our classrooms is the best way to ensure that when anyone observes our lessons, it is very clear that outstanding learning, over time, is typical. A closer look at the *September 2013 Ofsted Subsidiary Guidance,*[1] *Framework for School Inspection*[2] and *School Inspection Handbook*[3] can help you plan strategies to ensure that high expectations and great learning are embedded and become 'the way we always do things round here' – and not just for inspection day.

New focus

The latest updates to the *School Inspection Handbook* intend to put the focus on practices that make the most impact on

---

1 Ofsted, *Subsidiary Guidance*. Ref. 110166 (London: Ofsted, 2013).
2 Ofsted, *The Framework for School Inspection*. Ref. 120100 (London: Ofsted, 2013).
3 Ofsted, *School Inspection Handbook*. Ref. 120101 (London: Ofsted, 2013).

improving educational outcomes by making judgements on the following:

■ The achievement of pupils in the school.
■ The quality of teaching in the school.
■ The behaviour and safety of pupils at the school.
■ The quality of leadership in, and management of, the school.

At the same time, inspectors will also look at how well the school meets the needs of *all* pupils (see below) and how it promotes their spiritual, moral, social and cultural (SMSC) development to make a judgement on the 'overall effectiveness of the school'.

There will be a closer, focused scrutiny on the way the school meets the individual needs of students, such as those with disabilities, special educational needs (SEN), English as an additional language (EAL), young carers and those from low-income families. The pupil premium provides support for particular groups of children, such as looked-after children, children of service families and pupils eligible for free school meals. These children need to be making *at least* good progress for a school to be judged outstanding. Inspections will particularly scrutinise school results data over time for any potential underachievement amongst these groups and others such as boys, girls and ethnic minorities. In the 2013 Handbook, achievement of the 'most able' is mentioned several times, highlighting the concern about a lack of challenge for this group in some schools.[4]

For every classroom teacher, this means that vulnerable pupils need to be making rapid progress to close the gap and your most able pupils need to be effectively challenged. Consequently, you will need to have accurate information about what the school data shows. Who are the vulnerable groups in your school and have you got any of these pupils in your classes? Their names and needs should to be written in bold in your notebook and lesson plans so you get into the habit of ensuring that they are making good progress. Get into the habit of checking out if they need extra help or whether the most able need an additional challenge every lesson by talking to them, listening to them and watching them like a hawk!

Great teachers show they know the individual needs within each class (not just as a list) and have short- and long-term plans to monitor and meet them as they change. This may involve the use of additional resources, planned involvement of teaching assistants and quality oral and written feedback to pupils (and their parents). It may just be that bit of extra help or advice you give in the classroom or in the way you group them that makes the difference – but make sure you are aware of their learning journey and how well they are catching up – or, for the most able, leading the way.

The following list shows the types of behaviours it is useful to promote as often as possible:

---

4 See Ofsted, *School Inspection Handbook*, pp. 11, 15, 31, 32, 34, 35, 36, 37, 39 and 40.

Your pupils less often	Your pupils more often	Your pupils' work shows	Your classroom demonstrates
Are told what to do	Help decide what to aim for and how to go about it	Feedback shows strengths and specific advice to improve	Walls are used for learning, including displaying keywords or exemplars
Either know an answer or are left not knowing	Are shown exemplars and models of best work	Feedback is understood and acted on by the pupil	Some displays are interactive, such as a suggestions wall of ideas for future lessons
Are set objectives they don't understand or care about	Are engaged with the objectives and set their own success criteria	Pupils are interactive with their work	Quality work is displayed which is accurate in terms of spelling and presentation
Have to wait for feedback	Use their success criteria to reflect on and assess their work and progress	Work is improved over time and progress can be seen	
Are passive or coasting	Can use criteria to sum up what they have learned and seek feedback to act on immediately	Any targets/levels are understood	
Are formally assessed by an adult, scheme or authority	Really know how to improve		
	Have more feedback during their work than at the end and *do* something about it		
	Have time to reflect and act on feedback given		

cont

Your pupils less often	Your pupils more often	Your pupils' work shows	Your classroom demonstrates
Are assessed at the end of their work when it is too late to improve it	Know that critical feedback will help them improve	Care is taken with presentation, including dates and headings	Displays promote the good habits of great learners, such as resilience, empathy, using feedback, risk-taking, listening, collaborating and teamwork
Have little or no time to respond to feedback	Have support that helps them develop their own strategies and thinking skills	Work is accurate and completed	
Have levels or grades as a record of their progress and achievement	Make connections to previous learning and understand the relevance to planning further learning and activity	Work shows evidence of correction and practice	Wall displays encourage opportunities for reflection on success criteria and the learning journey
Peer assess inaccurately	Are developing a growth mindset and the habits of great learning	Work shows additional challenges are taken up	
	Peer and self-assess accurately and habitually	Pupils have taken care to follow up advice and feedback	Once a term, a wall is used to collect feedback from pupils (such as keep–change–grow)
	Are very ambitious and aspirational in their learning		

Chapter 3

Getting the core skills right

> There is excellent practice which ensures that all pupils have high levels of literacy appropriate to their age.
>
> Ofsted, *School Inspection Handbook* (2013): 29
>
> The teaching of reading, writing, communication and mathematics is highly effective and cohesively planned and implemented across the curriculum.
>
> Ofsted, *School Inspection Handbook* (2013): 39

It is entirely appropriate that there is an emphasis on core skills because without these skills, access to the rest of the curriculum is limited. The concern about lack of literacy in young people (even those who achieve GCSE English at C grade) has been well rehearsed recently. For years, we have been trying to give our students the skills to function well as employees and citizens, but all the statistics show that we have actually failed miserably; too many leave school lacking essential skills. As an English teacher working in both primary and secondary schools, I know the grind of trying to teach reading, writing and numeracy skills to reluctant learners who already believe they can't.

A single literacy or numeracy coordinator in schools who simply ensures subject keywords are put up in every classroom will no longer suffice. Teaching core skills is not a job just for the English or maths departments either. Every teacher in every lesson must make a contribution to improving them. The core skills must be *taught and modelled* right across the curriculum. We need to be more creative and ambitious in creating strategies that improve these skills in new and exciting ways, in every classroom, from reception to Year 13. An exciting, ongoing, rigorous literacy and numeracy drive (starting with the teachers) affecting every aspect of school life must aim for better outcomes. This means building more of a hearts-and-minds determination by students and teachers to first value and then develop core skills.

Focus on literacy in every lesson

Literacy is the core skill that can and should be taught and modelled in every lesson. In primary schools it permeates every lesson. In secondary schools the development of literacy will be expected in every subject. Delivering progress in literacy in your lesson will be expected if you are to be rated 'outstanding'. This means taking every opportunity to improve the communication skills of your pupils. It doesn't mean squeezing an extra activity into a packed schedule – it means raising awareness of these skills in what you are already delivering.

Mindset tweak

You are the expert learner – don't be afraid of admitting mistakes or letting the pupils correct your spelling or grammar. Admit you are still learning and that it really matters to get it right!

First, try to ensure that your own literacy skills are as perfect as possible. Check your spelling and grammar in every PowerPoint or written word you place on the board or wall. Get into the habit of getting it right every time. Get the pupils to check out your spelling, grammar and correct you if they can. This is modelling 'every mistake is a learning experience'! We all make mistakes and get it wrong sometimes, but the important thing is we know what is right and always strive to be accurate. There are no excuses – you must model a determination to be an accurate, effective, flexible communicator if you want to be an excellent teacher. If you worry about your literacy or numeracy skills, don't hide it and wait to be caught out – insist on some training and keep on learning.

Grammatical errors heard during lesson observations:

'We was just going to start the activity …'

'Look at them wonderful mountains!'

'Was you wanting to do it now or later?'

'You can take them books home for research.'

'I could of told you that.'

Every time you teach a lesson and focus on applying literacy and numeracy skills, you will be improving your own literacy and numeracy. Enjoying the wonder of words and numbers in your lesson is the very best way to help your pupils feel confident about developing their own literacy and numeracy.

Building a 'literate' lesson: action to take

- Build literacy awareness into your lesson plan.
- Introduce and celebrate new vocabulary (not just subject-related words).
- Value reading and encourage reading aloud in class, paired and privately. Set reading homework and check it is done. Show the pupils books or magazines you are reading at the moment.
- Give wider subject reading suggestions, including relevant magazines.
- Give tips on paragraphing, spelling, punctuation and grammar.
- Reward literacy skills used in your lessons.
- Encourage the use of Standard English rigorously, both spoken and written. When it is appropriate not to use it, say why – for example, when role play requires an accent or dialect. There should be no judgement about accents or dialects, just an understanding that Standard English is a useful form to use in certain situations such as exams and interviews.
- Reinforce grammatical accuracy in spoken language – for example, correcting 'We was ...' and 'Them books ...'
- Use texting, blogs, Twitter and email to engage their communication skills in your subject and demonstrate the different qualities of various forms of communication.

- Care about literacy skills in your lesson – offer prizes for students who catch you out making a mistake and model mistakes as learning experiences.
- Remind students about writing in good, clear sentences and paragraphs – if you show you value this, they will value it too.
- Look out for students who are not reading very much because others in the group are doing it for them.
- Mark spellings and give spelling tests for subject-related words.
- Give students an opportunity to assess their writing skills using a simple grid whenever they do any written work (see Appendix 5).
- Ensure that key terms and vocabulary are clear and relate them to similar words or their root.
- Give regular advice on spelling and punctuation strategies.
- Enhance skills in skimming and scanning text for information.
- Explain writing conventions as part of your delivery – for example, writing to inform or persuade.

Finally, have you ever noticed that some students do not like to read and write? They are the very students who need to read and write more often in your lesson. More reading and more writing is crucial for improvement in literacy.

Numeracy is more difficult to incorporate regularly, but don't miss any opportunity to make using numbers in a practical way part of what you do. For example, get them to work out how many groups of three we will have in the class or how much it costs to feed a family for a week.

Ingredients of an outstanding lesson

A prompt start to learning is crucial for great lessons, so get your pupils into the habit of knowing there is always an interesting mystery or challenge to get on with when they arrive and are waiting for everyone else. In fact, make it so much fun that they race to get there and you have no problems with punctuality and behaviour as they come into your room. Rewards for completing the 'greeting' task can be leadership roles they enjoy, books or magazines to take home, medals to wear for the lesson, choosing the music for the interval task or, for older children, credits/merits towards book vouchers or use of technology in breaktimes.

Mindset tweak

Choose the most challenging student and make a connection with them as soon as they walk in – for example, say 'You're going to have the best lesson ever today!'

Greeting tasks can be related to the lesson objective. Here are some examples:

■ A set of pictures and/or words are on the table which represent the learning for the lesson and which will be used later. The greeting challenge is to arrange them in the right order.

- An object that relates to the lesson objective is on each desk. The pair of students with the best explanation in ten words about the connection wins.
- A question is on the board. Pupils have to think of three follow-up questions.
- A rucksack (or picture of one) is empty. Pupils have to fill it with six things they need for making today's learning journey successful.
- An anagram that relates to learning from last lesson has to be decoded.
- The objective is on the board and the pupils have to work out the success criteria.
- The objective is on the board and children have to work out three ways in which this piece of learning will be important in their lives.
- The teacher could be wearing a costume or a wig and the pupils have to work out why it is relevant to this lesson.

The greeting task should be quick and only take a few moments as children are arriving at your lesson. Eventually they can design their own greeting tasks.

Engagement – priming the brain

Though not essential, a starter activity can prime the brain so that the learning sticks. The first activity can either close down or open up possibilities for learning. It can fix a mind-set of 'I can't do this' or nurture a state of curiosity and wonder. The primacy effect occurs in the first six seconds and means that initial impressions are powerful and hard to shift later. It also means that the first six seconds of an inspector's visit to your classroom will be influential. Getting brains actively engaged immediately will pay massive dividends. A class enthusiastically and quickly involved in learning is very impressive and, having finished the greeting task, the children will now be readier to engage with the lesson objectives and the success criteria.

Engaging pupils with lesson objectives: questions to ask

1. What will change if we meet this objective?

2. What questions do you want to ask about this objective?

3. How will we really know we have met it?

4. Can you find ten crazy ways to show me you have succeeded in this objective?

5. What is the first thing I need to do this lesson?

Don't slow the pace by making them all tediously write the objective down. Instead:

- Provide it on a piece of paper.
- Get them to pick out and write down the keywords from the objective.
- Write the objective in 'text speak' at the beginning of the lesson, leaving gaps for other letters. At the end, fill in the gaps – making it a good literacy reflection too!
- Try spacing out the words so at the end of the lesson they can see if they can fill in the gaps or decide that they should have chosen different keywords.
- Make the objective into a diagram/picture or emoticon. This is a great way to check they know what is on the learning journey and why.
- Simply start the lesson and then ask them to guess the objective later on.

It is important to ring the changes and break out of your usual routine of PowerPoint, lesson objective, activate, demonstrate, plenary. Change can be effective for securing engagement and keeping the pupils alert and in learning mode.

Mindset tweak: self-evaluation

When you are moving around the classroom checking understanding and progress, ask pupils what the objective was and what they have done that has helped them make good progress. Especially ask the pupil premium and most able learners.

Challenge and feedback

It's not enough to say your expectations are high – you have to encourage a culture within your classroom that says, 'In here we all support each other to work outside our comfort zones'.

Working in their comfort zone is nice because nothing is too taxing. It makes pupils feel good because they aren't stretched, frustrated or just bored with the repetition and practice needed to master some tasks. However, for our learners to make outstanding progress they sometimes need to feel the pain to make the gain. Yes, we can make it fun and find new strategies to ease the pain but, sometimes, learning new information or skills is hard and pupils will feel uncomfortable. Do you remember trying to learn to play the piano or ballroom dancing or how use a new type of computer?

Some of our most challenging learners have already decided that when learning gets hard it is best avoided because it makes them feel bad when they can't do things. The dyslexic child will read and write less – but needs to read and write more. Practice and practice and more practice is what creates genius – 10,000 hours of practice, according to Malcolm Gladwell.[5] When learning gets tough, that's when pupils are acquiring new skills and mustn't give up or step back.

So, how can we help our students to love a challenge and stick at it, even when it's hard? They 'simply' need to get into the habit of working hard, getting stuck and unstuck – and getting a real kick out of it – because that is what you've taught them is normal in your class. Pupils find an intrinsic satisfaction in succeeding after working hard. This is very important to nurture in our vulnerable learners who may not have such role models at home.

Checklist: working beyond the comfort zone

- Do your students know what their 'comfort' and 'challenge' zones are and that when they work in the challenge zone they will make good progress?
- Have they got into the habit of pushing themselves when it gets hard or dull?
- Do they understand that some learning needs lots of repetition to get it right?
- Do they know how to use strategies, such as using rhyme and visual imagery, to help them learn important facts and formulas?

---

5 M. Gladwell, *Outliers: The Story of Success* (London: Penguin, 2008), p. 35.

- Do your teaching assistants regularly encourage persistence and resilience in learning – effectively?
- Are your 'most able' pupils regularly given the extra challenge they need?
- Do they challenge themselves to work beyond their target levels?
- Have you got mantras that will help remind them of the above (e.g. 'When the going gets tough, the tough get going' or 'Every mistake is a learning experience')?

Mindset tweak

Are you expecting enough of them? Try something extraordinarily challenging and see what happens. For example, put your most able pupils in front of the class and get them to do some of the teaching ...

Feedback for differentiation

Having high expectations of pupils with various needs requires an accurate assessment of the barriers to their learning, then making effective interventions to help them make good progress. This entails giving pupils pertinent written and oral feedback against success criteria. Research has found effective feedback to be one of the most profound and power-ful ways to close the gap for underachievers.[6]

> Teachers systematically and effectively check pupils' understanding throughout lessons, anticipating where they may need to intervene and doing so with notable impact on the quality of learning.
>
> Ofsted, *School Inspection Handbook* (2013): 39

Feedback during the lesson should be tailored to achieve the most powerful effect for each pupil. It could be a comment, question, demonstration, correction of error, scaffolding, coaching or example. You must relentlessly assess how well your feedback is working – ask the pupils what works!

Oral or written feedback that is specific and positive and that guides students to make progress in their learning journey is both developmental and motivational. Your lesson should be full of it. The more immediate feedback is, the more powerful it can be, so the way you talk to learners when they are learn-ing will help them to make good progress.

---

6   See Higgins et al., *Toolkit of Strategies to improve Learning* and Hattie, *Visible Learning for Teachers*.

Mindset tweak

Teach pupils to really understand the importance of feedback – and how they can make logical, objective responses to it. Reinforce feedback as 'the breakfast of champions' by looking at the way sports stars use it.

Watch and really listen to learn what works in the classroom to help individuals make progress. Continually adapt your language, body language, questions, ideas and advice until you get a positive result.

Feedback in books and on pupils' work is also essential to record and demonstrate the way learning is progressing over time. You should be able to look at pupils' work and clearly see how your specific guidance and advice has been acknowledged, acted upon and helped to support progress. When you mark books, ensure that pupils read and respond to the feedback you have given by building DIRT time into your lesson. Southam College, in Warwickshire uses a consistent method to do this called FAR:

Feedback: A brief comment praising effort and, if required, judging outcome level.

Action: Specific advice on what they need to do next to improve.

Response: Pupils complete the suggested actions then sign this section with a comment if appropriate.

Great feedback will:

1. Focus on the learning objectives, outcome and/or success criteria.

2. Stimulate the correction of errors or improvement of a piece of work.

3. Scaffold or support pupils' next steps.

4. Comment on progress over a number of attempts.

5. Provide opportunities for pupils to think things through for themselves and *respond* as soon as possible.

6. Make it imperative that they *do* something different to improve.

7. Focus on *effort, progress* and *process* so that pupils become 'assessment capable'.

8. Encourage creating their own challenges to make the next steps for learning.

Which of the following will help your pupils make more progress?

Descriptive comments in books will be a waste of your time if they are not read or acted on. Make comments imperative. Example H should say 'Rewrite the ending' and Example D could say 'Replace five words with more interesting words' so that pupils have to respond in or before the next lesson.

C – Oral (teacher)

The effort that you are putting in is really starting to pay off

F – Oral (teacher)

*What else can you try
What has worked before?*

B – Written (teacher)

96% – a brilliant score that you deserve

E – Oral (teacher)

Your take off was excellent, Matt. On your next jump try to have a more graceful landing

H – Written (teacher)

B – Good start but your answer deteriorated towards the end

A – Oral (teacher)

Your answers are spot on – keep this up

D – Written (teacher)

C – Great effort. You need more detail and use of exciting vocabulary

G – Oral (teacher)

You made good eye-contact with your partner. Very supportive body language. Don't forget to smile

Focusing solely on outcomes, results or grades, as in examples A and B, makes pupils less likely to try something harder next time in case they do less well – which they can see as 'failing'. Beware of using grades before a comment, as in D – the grade is all that may get read.

Example F will only work when pupils have been trained to self-assess and really understand the progress levels and what they need to do to improve. However, this type of coaching question is powerful for developing thinking and for encouraging pupils to own their own progress.

Example G uses praise and specific advice very well and the teacher can check it is put into action immediately in the next attempt.

Questioning

Asking questions is the bread and butter of teaching and they are the lifeblood of outstanding learning. The very best teachers ask questions that help learners make connections and move their thinking forward. This type of questioning means being patient and responsive, in order to build on their answers so that understanding is truly deepened.

Using questions to develop learning and help students make progress in their thinking is a subject in itself. Good, open and engaging questions promote thinking at the highest levels of Bloom's Taxonomy.[7] Questions such as 'why', 'how' and

---

7 For information on Bloom's Taxonomy of learning domains visit http://www. nwlink.com/~donclark/hrd/bloom.html (accessed 11 September 2013).

'what if' are the basic tools of teaching that push a learner's thinking towards the higher order skills in Bloom's Taxonomy where they are seeking to evaluate information rather than just learn it.

However, we should also make students formulate more of their own questions more often, encourage thinking time for questions and use Socratic questioning to regularly create a community of enquiry.[8] In our knowledge-based economy, where access to digital information is freely available, we need to train our pupils to be discerning and able to see 'grey' areas and all sides of an argument. Critical questioning will challenge all learners to evaluate issues, deepen their understanding and help embed knowledge.

Socratic questioning

Socratic questioning is at the heart of critical thinking and using these types of open questions in the classroom, and for homework, will help you promote deeper learning:

1. **Questions for clarification:**
   - Why do you say that?
   - How does this relate to our discussion?
   - Are you going to include your working out in your equations?

---

8   For information on Philosophy for Children visit http://www.sapere.org.uk/.

2. **Questions that probe assumptions:**
   - What else could be causing this?
   - How can you find out if that is true?
   - Why are you using the same source to get your evidence as last time?

3. **Questions that probe reasons and evidence:**
   - What would be an example?
   - What is ... similar to?
   - What do you think ... causes ... to happen? Why?
   - Do you think that exercise will always make you fit?

4. **Questions about viewpoints and perspectives:**
   - What would be an alternative?
   - What is another way to look at it?
   - Would you explain why it is necessary and who benefits?
   - What are the strengths and weaknesses of ...?
   - How are ... and ... similar?
   - How could we prevent traffic jams and would this be good for everyone?

5. **Questions that probe implications and consequences:**

- What generalisations can you make?
- What are the consequences of that assumption?
- What are you implying?
- How does ... affect ...?
- How does ... connect with what we learned before?
- What would happen if you didn't come to school?

6. **Questions about the question:**

- What was the point of this question?
- Why do you think I asked this question?
- How does ... apply to everyday life?
- Why do you need to learn this?

These questions deepen knowledge and challenge pupils. The very best teachers should know the level of progress each answer represents.

Questioning that promotes and probes thinking

Teacher: John, what makes you think that photosynthesis is vital for our planet?

John: Because nothing could live.

Teacher: Why would nothing live?

John: Well, the process makes life possible.

Teacher: How does photosynthesis make life possible? Jenny, help him out ...

Jenny: Is it because plants take in carbon dioxide and water and produce oxygen?

Teacher: How does that help us?

Jenny: Plants use the CO_2 and H_2O to make sugars using energy from the sun to do it. They can then combine the sugars with minerals from the ground to make all the chemicals that plants, and the animals that eat them, need to live and grow. The oxygen is produced as a by-product of photosynthesis but is useful for plant and animal respiration.

Teacher: Excellent Jenny! Now can you help show John how this works using a diagram?

Asking these Socratic, coaching-type questions encourages thinking and pupil dialogue in a lesson and, as the average verbal expression for a student in a secondary classroom is only five words,[9] this has to be a priority. The questions students ask can also act as a form of plenary to measure learning.

The beauty of students constructing questions instead of lots of answers is that questions, unlike answers, cannot easily be defined as right or wrong, giving them a freedom to explore and deepen learning. For example, 'Think of three questions this article raises' and 'Tell me three things you have learned from this article' both measure progress but feel different to closed questions.

Mindset tweak

Encouraging pupils to frame questions for you will help them to develop a language for learning related to your subject.

The questions you ask in your classroom and the confidence with which your pupils formulate their own questions are powerful levers for learning.

---

9 J. West Burnham and M. Coates, *Transforming Education for Every Child: A Practical Handbook* (London: Network Educational Press, 2006), quoted in C. Gadsby, *The Perfect Assessment for Learning* (Carmarthen: Crown House Publishing, 2012), p. 36.

Teachers listen to, carefully observe and skilfully question pupils during lessons in order to reshape tasks and explanations to improve learning.

Ofsted, *School Inspection Handbook* (2013): 39

Top tips

Plan your lessons by writing down the key questions to be answered and link these to levels of progression or exam grades.

Use Bloom's Taxonomy to ensure your questions are challenging their thinking:

Remembering – understanding – applying – analysing – evaluating – creating

- Get into the habit of asking coaching-type, Socratic questions that make pupils think for themselves – for example, 'What do you think will happen next if you do that?'

- Allow thinking time and paired thinking to better explore possible answers and engage more pupils.

- Use mini whiteboards or electronic devices to enable *all* pupils to attempt to answer questions.

- Be relentless and fearless in follow-up questions to draw out the learning.
- Welcome unexpected answers and build on them to reconstruct your lesson.
- Respond to wrong answers by showing they are an excellent addition to our learning journey!
- Encourage pupils to pose their own questions – set this as homework.
- Always ask of yourself and the pupils: 'How will learning this be useful in your life outside school?'

Independent and collaborative learning

Spoon-fed students who have not developed research or thinking skills and who have been towed through tests develop a learned helplessness that will come back and bite them in higher education or the world of work.

Pupils develop and apply a wide range of skills to great effect in reading, writing, communication and mathematics. They are exceptionally well prepared for the next stage in their education, training or employment.

Ofsted, *School Inspection Handbook* (2013): 35

Doing it for them is often quicker and easier than making them do it for themselves, but the very best teachers make independent learning a priority and a principle. Deeper learning needs the purpose of the learning explained and requires active engagement and involvement with the material to make proper progress.

So, what is independent learning? The teacher is the expert and has the knowledge and experience to share. A teacher passionately imparting knowledge and inspiring enthusiasm by telling pupils about a topic or strategy can be a very effective teaching technique. However, the next stage must involve pupils using that knowledge and applying it in new ways, maybe collaboratively, to ensure they understand it and can use it. This is how we deepen the learning. Some lessons need to include independent learning time which reviews and challenges their understanding. The pupils must be aware that they need to work on their own or with others to solve problems, find solutions, evaluate new information, link it to prior learning and produce an outcome that relates to the learning objective.

One of the most effective ways to deepen and embed learning is to teach others what you have just learnt. This encourages communication skills and cognitive development. 'Peer learning' was recommended as another of those powerful ways to close the gap for underachievers in research that identified the most cost-effective ways to add value in the classroom.[10]

---

10 Higgins et al., *Toolkit of Strategies to Improve Learning*, p. 5.

Children, especially those from underprivileged backgrounds, need to learn how to communicate, influence, negotiate and network. This is something the public sector knows very well, as outlined in Mick Waters' thought-provoking book on schooling over the last 20 years: 'Children need to know how to make contacts and use them to build up networks that they can enjoy, exploit and benefit from.'[11]

Creating lessons where pupils are encouraged to constantly challenge their communication skills by acting out roles and working in dynamic teams will help them to be flexible and adaptable.

Student leadership roles

Assigning leadership roles to various pupils in the classroom helps them take more responsibility for the progress of all. The cards below can be made into badges and will ensure pupils are consciously focusing on developing certain aspects of their learning.

PROGRESS CHECKER Makes sure we are making progress towards our learning outcome	NUMERACY AMBASSADOR Looks for any way we can use parts of the lesson to improve our understanding of numbers

---

11 Waters, *Thinking Allowed on Schooling*, p. 46.

LITERACY AMBASSADOR	LEAD GREETER
Looks for any literacy mistakes, keywords or brilliant vocabulary to celebrate	Greets any visitor by explaining what we are doing and how far we have got
LEAD CELEBRATOR	LEAD QUESTIONER
Celebrates good things they have seen in the lesson	Asks a really good question to help us all understand a little bit more: how, what and why
GROWTH MINDSET GURU	LEARNING TO LEARN ASSESSOR
Makes sure we are all becoming more emotionally intelligent by pushing ourselves out of our comfort zones and showing a positive attitude	Reports on how the class has been learning – what is working and what isn't

Case study: Year 5 literacy

As you walk into Sue Ware's lesson at King John Middle School, in Northamptonshire, there is a buzz of activity with 26 children grouped around tables working on various literacy tasks according to their current targets and individual needs.

One group, mainly boys, are working with the teacher using tablets, discovering various tools and apps to improve their spelling. The group I spoke to about their learning were the middle ability group who were working on what can only be described as very challenging words and phrases to extend their vocabulary. On the table were laminated quotes like 'All thinking begins with wondering' and 'Apply past knowledge to new situations'. Pupils could explain what these meant and why they were relevant in each case.

Each child also had a badge. Suddenly the music for *Pink Panther* came on for a few seconds and those with the Learning Spy badge were off on their mission to 'spy' on other groups' good ideas to help them with their own group tasks. When asked if they resented someone stealing their work, the indignant reply was, 'Well, that's how we learn – from each other and by trying new ideas out.' Other badges for class leadership included Ogre (peer assessor), Word Monster (the scribe), Brain Teaser (who develops flexible thinking habits) and ii, which also had a picture of two eyes (for the pupil given the job of being the work checker).

What was most impressive was the way these roles were acted out with conviction and understanding – as if interdependent learning was just part of what they always do.

The lowest ability group, which had been working on iPads, were then tasked to teach the others in small groups about how to use the app Word Mess to extend their skills in spelling and vocabulary.

The quality of the work in books was as high as I have seen in Year 9 English lessons, and the marking supported progress with feedback that helped pupils focus on how to improve. Some wonderful writing, completed as an 'Ogre report', was adventurous and exciting.

The pupils I spoke to were impressively articulate about their learning and how they could improve. It was clear that they understood levels and progress and were also encouraged to have an active engagement with their learning journey.

We paused as the teacher gathered pupils on the mat and checked out prior learning about an author's writing that had been set as homework. A line of baby pictures across the top of the wall was used as a continuum for assessing their starting point for the task. This was a fun way to consider how much the pupils thought they knew and clearly was used regularly. Music was then used for children to move from one table to another, swapping and growing their factual knowledge about the author and her work. Each time the music stopped the pupils moved on and shared another new fact that then had to be explained to the next person.

One pupil then gave a PowerPoint presentation he had put together as his homework, extending the knowledge about the author and books she had written. He finished this with an interactive quiz for the class to check what they had learnt from his session! Finally, following examples of examining and analysing the writing style, pupils attempted an extended writing task of their own.

The strengths of this lesson emerged from the embedded learning skills demonstrated by what each child said and did in the short time I was there. They could articulate what they were doing, knew how they could improve and what strategies they could use when stuck. All ability levels were challenged and excited about their learning. On the wall was a suggestions and reflections board where pupils could put forward their ideas for how things could be improved in future lessons.

Some comments from pupils about their teacher were: 'She tells us exactly what we need to improve on', 'She makes us practice so that we remember and never give up', 'It's always fun and she is very kind', 'We all work together to make sure everyone does well in this class – it doesn't matter which group you are in' and 'She wants to prove to the Headteacher that tablets work for spelling!'

Sue's motivation for teaching is that she wants to create a hunger for learning in her class where children always want to improve. She believes that whatever their starting point they can always make progress. What makes it all worthwhile for her is seeing one of her most challenging students swell with pride, grow and change as he finds ways to make learning work for him and break through his learning barriers.

In this lesson, Sue hardly spoke but the learning and achievement shown by her pupils in the lesson and over time, as shown in their books, demonstrated outstanding progress.

What about the new curriculum?

There will be a new national curriculum soon – there will always be a *new* national curriculum; but actually the curriculum is the child's complete experience of learning at school – including assemblies, lunch breaks, lessons, sports practice, trips, visits and so on.

> The important thing to remember is that, in an English school, teachers can teach their children anything as long as it is legal and safe.
>
> Mick Waters[12]

We will always have a list of content to teach and a set of tests to take, but how you deliver the content and what the

12 Waters, *Thinking Allowed on Schooling*, p. 267.

children experience in your classroom is your responsibility, meaning that the power is always in your hands. You can make your principles and values clear as you teach those vital learning habits to your pupils, reminding them during every activity how important it is to take risks, create solutions, welcome feedback, communicate with empathy, push yourself outside your comfort zone and ask good questions.

> Unless you are completely sick and tired of talking about your message, you aren't even close to getting your audience to adopt it.
>
> Patty Azzarello[13]

Developing these habits requires frequent, active, collaborative learning. Group projects can really encourage and promote independent learning, especially if they involve choice, challenge and a competitive element. We all know that extra-curricular learning often creates some of the most powerful memories, emotions and experiences a pupil will ever have during their school lives. School productions can involve learning boring lines, waiting for hours to go on, wearing silly clothes and huge performance anxiety, but pupils also learn skills they will never forget. Sports teams practise for hours, requiring extra time and effort outside of normal classes, but pupils choose to take part, motivate themselves and commit to making progress. Why? Because the power of teamwork and the challenge involved in producing a positive

---

13 P. Azzarello, *Rise* (Palo Alto, CA: Ten Speed Press, 2010), p. 33.

outcome are highly motivational. Often, the pupils who take part in these activities also become more successful in everything else.

Pupil led challenge projects

> When you provide them with some choice over how to demonstrate their learning, however small it may be, you reduce the emphasis on performance or surface learning and increase the emphasis on mastery of subject or deep learning.
>
> James M. Lang[14]

Here are some ideas for collaborative activities that replicate some of the features of sports and drama activities (more can be found at www.jackiebeere.com). Build your collaborative work around giving your pupils a choice of activities, letting them set their own guided success criteria and earning points for their team.

---

14 J. M. Lang, *Cheating Lessons: Learning from Academic Dishonesty* (Cambridge, MA: Harvard University Press, 2013), quoted in *TES*, 30 August 2013.

Year 6/7: English

Learning outcome: You will have a deeper understanding of characters and themes in your book

Choose a task to complete to deepen your understanding of a character in the book

1. Describe appearance – facial expressions, body language, clothes, etc.

2. Write the character's favourite sayings for different occasions

3. Describe their perfect weekend away with a full list of activities

4. Prepare a music playlist for your character with reasons for your choices

5. Write a Facebook profile and some comments for their wall

6. Imagine your character ten years from now and write about how their life has turned out

7. Design a logo and motto for your character

8. Write a blog as if you were the character and giving his/her views on a recent news story

9. Write a magazine interview of your character

10. Write the letter from the character's mum or dad giving advice

11. Write a short play script starring your character – be prepared to perform it

12. Create your own task – check it out with your teacher

Year 11/12: Biology

Prepare a 40 minute lesson on your topic to teach the rest of the class

Learning outcome: The whole class will be able to interpret pressure and volume data and ECG trace. Each group/pair will research one of these areas and prepare and teach a 40 minute lesson on it

Heart beat

2. **The functions of the mammalian circulatory system and the structure of its parts**

Artery, vein, capillary, arterioles, double circulation

3. **Heart structure**

Prepare labelled dissections and draw diagrams to show the atria, ventricles, left and right aortic valves, septum, aorta, pulmonary artery and vein, vena cava, coronary artery

4. **Design and carry out experiments** to investigate resting pulse rate, rate during exercise, recovery time. Include cardiac output

1. **Heart disease and its causes**

Hypertension, atheroma, cholesterol, aneurysm, thrombosis, angina, arrhythmia, coronary cardiovascular disease, myocardial infarction

5. **Control of the beat**

Cardiac cycle, autonomic system, vagus, myogenic contraction, atrioventricular node, sinuatrial node, Purkinje fibres/bundle of His, wave of activity

You can fill in the gaps, correct any mistakes and build on the learning presented by the pupils in the above activity.

Mindset tweak

Have high expectations as pupils will often surprise you with what they can achieve.

Top tips

Create a culture in your classroom that values and promotes independent learning – e.g. techniques such as 3B4ME (meaning pupils try three strategies before asking the teacher).

Try to make sure that 70% of your lesson consists of active, collaborative learning.

Encourage pupils to teach and present to each other as often as possible.

If children work in groups, ensure that all have roles and none are passengers.

Create projects and activities that include choice, challenge and competition in order to really motivate them to work independently.

Give pupils varied leadership roles that will challenge their comfort zones and help them take responsibility for class progress.

Make sure teaching assistants always encourage children to do the work for themselves as much as possible.

Give the pupils the success criteria so they can assess their own progress regularly and understand what they need to do next.

Mind the gap: progress for all and closing the learning gap – rapidly

The standards of attainment of almost all groups of pupils are likely to be at least in line with national averages with many pupils attaining above this. In exceptional circumstances, an outstanding grade can be awarded where standards of attainment of any group of pupils are below those of all pupils nationally, but the gap is closing rapidly, as shown by trends in a range of attainment indicators.

Ofsted, *School Inspection Handbook* (2013): 35

Seeing engaged, resilient, ambitious learners working independently in the classroom on challenging activities and making good or outstanding progress is one mark of an out-standing lesson. Make sure also that you know where the attainment gaps in your school are and that you plan every lesson to help underperforming pupils make extra progress. School leaders should regularly track underperforming groups of students across their whole school experience and feedback to you how much impact you are making with these pupils, so that you can adjust and adapt your teaching.

Ensuring progress for all: action to improve the use of teaching assistants

You may be lucky enough to have teaching assistants employed to specifically help and support pupils. However, beware: the quality of your teaching will be judged by the impact your teaching assistants have on your vulnerable learners. You need to plan their interventions and make sure they promote progress in thinking and learning. Research has shown that some teaching assistants tend to babysit or do the work for their students. The skills and range of strategies for learning that teaching assistants need to help reluctant learn-ers make outstanding progress and work independently are *very* challenging to acquire. It is in your and your school's interest to train up your teaching assistants.

Inspectors must evaluate the use of, and contribution made by, teaching assistants.

Ofsted, *School Inspection Handbook* (2013): 37

Ensure that your teaching assistants know and understand the objectives of the lesson – and how they relate to the students they are working with – and plan the teaching assistant's input, making a note of this in your lesson plan. You should also keep a record of the way teaching assistants are contributing to learning over time to help you plan their use more effectively across the school.

Additionally, ensure that your teaching assistants:

- Understand progression in your subject area and how to scaffold it.
- Have a way to feed back to the teacher the successes and failures of the learning – linked to the objectives of that lesson.
- Can mark and set targets linked to progression and objectives for their students.
- Help students to set success criteria and understand exactly what they need to do.
- Can assess and observe – giving their students one-to-one feedback that really works.
- Believe they can make a difference to progress.
- Are extra eyes and ears in class, identifying progress problems and suggesting strategies to the teacher.
- Are fully trained in a range of alternative learning strategies.

Assessment as learning

> Question: With pupil progress being at the heart of an outstanding lesson, how can we show this when observed for only 25 minutes?
>
> Answer: The progress of your pupils over time will be the key indicator and this will be judged by your lesson, scrutinising books and talking to pupils.

Proof that your students are making this amazing progress includes:

- How well and frequently marking, assessment and testing are used to help teachers improve pupils' learning.
- The level of challenge provided.
- Pupils' effort and success in completing their work, responding to feedback and the progress made over a period of time.

So, making assessment an integral part of the learning process through regular target-setting, sharing success criteria, self-assessment, peer assessment, mini tests and quizzes, and regular marking and feedback that is acted on is essential. Hattie says: 'Students who have developed their assessment capabilities are more able and motivated to access, interpret, and use information from quality assessments in ways that affirm or further their learning.'[15] To do this and become confident reviewers of their learning journey, they need opportunities to reflect, amend and improve in DIRT time.

Great teachers will also train their pupils to give and take constructive criticism without losing confidence in order to become resilient learners.

Mindset tweak

Skim through your pupils' books regularly. Can you see the progress they have made in the last six months? Has your marking made a difference? Make a note of anything you learn from this as part of your self-evaluation process.

Subject progress

Teachers need to be very clear about the progression model for their subject and how each lesson fits in with it. Exactly what skills and knowledge are needed for pupils to improve? Then let's do the activity that delivers those skills and that knowledge. It is so important for learners to know exactly what they are trying to learn and how to recognise when they are making good progress. This involves explicit sharing of success criteria so pupils will know how to measure their

---

15 Hattie, *Visible Learning for Teachers*, p. 126.

achievements. Research has shown that this is one of the most effective assessment for learning strategies.

The 8 Schools Project

The 8 Schools Project investigated exactly what helps pupils make more progress. One of the report's key messages is that: 'Pupils' progress is accelerated when they are clear about the success criteria for the intended outcomes and are able to judge the quality of their work and know how to improve it. This requires teachers having a good understanding of pro-gression in the key concepts and skills in their subject.'[16]

Learning happens in pupils' heads as they assess their level of understanding or quality of their work and recognise how to improve it. If they can understand the level they are work-ing at and what they need to do (exactly) to move forward, then learners will make more progress. As Claire Gadsby says in her excellent guide, *Perfect Assessment for Learning*: 'We need to be much more explicit about our expectations of pupils by the active sharing and, where possible, genuine co-construc-tion of success criteria with them.'[17]

You (and your students) must be very clear about how to progress in your subject. You could use a continuum model to show students the different levels or steps along their learning journey. From this, they can work out their starting points and where they need to go. This model is described in

---

16 Department for Education and Skills, *Assessment for Learning 8 Schools Project Report* (London: DfES, 2007), p. 12.
17 Gadsby, *Perfect Assessment for Learning*, p. 29.

The Perfect Ofsted Lesson (Beere, 2010) and has been adapted by teachers into a learning ladder, road trip or learning wheel to encourage metacognition about the process and progress of learning and how it works (see Chapter 1 and below).

A classroom display that shows the learning progress as a journey and which gives pupils a model to reflect on in terms of where they are going, what potholes they may meet on the way, what the destination is, how they can travel faster and so on, is a useful tool. This can become a regular topic of conversation and encourages metacognition and discussion about progress.

Learning ladder for progress in maths

Lucy Westley is a Key Stage 2 teacher, leading Teaching and Learning at Tiffield Primary School, in Northamptonshire. She has developed some very useful learning ladders for children to record their progress against levels that describe what they can do. In the grid below, children can tick off their multiplication skills, plus there is a teacher box to verify the step has been achieved. The colours signify different ability levels.

Learning ladder for multiplication

	Step	Child	Teacher
1	Can I use an appropriate non-calculator method to multiply any 3 digit number by any 2 digit number?		
2	Can I solve balancing sums involving multiplication?		
3	Can I use brackets within a multiplication?		
4	Can I use a chosen method to multiply a simple decimal by a single digit number?		

	Step	Child	Teacher
5	Can I use the compact vertical method for multiplication (2 digit x 2 digit)?		
6	Can I use the vertical method for multiplication (2 digit x 2 digit)?		
7	Can I use the grid method (using partitioning) to multiply a 2 digit number by a 2 digit number?		
8	Can I use the grid method to multiply a 2 digit number by a single digit number?		
9	Can I multiply a single digit number by a multiple of 10?		
10	Can I use arrays as a step into the grid method?		

For more detailed examples of the working method for these stages visit www.jackiebeere.com.

Know your impact by the end of the lesson

The best plenary is the one that shows you and the pupils how much they have learnt and how much progress you *all* have made. It may not come right at the end, it may consist of many mini plenaries, but look on it as your scoreboard and your ultimate feedback. Involve *all* the pupils in this process by testing what they now know with:

- A test or quiz
- Using mini whiteboards to write down answers
- Putting three things they have learnt on sticky notes
- Writing Twitter messages of ten words or less to sum up the learning
- Chanting what they have learnt
- Pair sharing what they now know
- Creating a question/quiz for you
- Designing a lesson logo

Use metaphors, such as a rucksack into which they put notes showing the useful things they learned today and will need for the next part of their journey. Innovative learning strategies, new skills or amazing vocabulary they can use again can go into a treasure chest and any bits they are stuck on or questions they still have about the lesson can go into a first-aid box.

Measuring progress – the perfect plenary happens throughout ...

What do we need for the next part of the journey?

This process lets you find out whether they have achieved the learning outcome – or not. However, you will have a pretty good idea about how they are doing because you will have been swooping in on their work and checking learning progress throughout the lesson. There are plenty of great books full of plenary ideas to try, but the main thing is that you must make sure that this activity really does tell you what you need to know at the end of the lesson: did they (especially the gap pupils) really get it?

Top tips

Remember the primacy effect – engage the pupils from the very start. Don't waste learning time waiting for others to arrive.

Have a regular, exciting challenge/starter activity ready.

Ensure it is a brain primer, making them curious and believing they can achieve.

Engage the pupils with your success criteria by making them real and relevant to them.

Make progress your mantra – make sure pupils know how your objectives will deliver this by co-designing the success criteria with them.

Have high expectations and make sure they love being challenged because they know it works.

Ensure vulnerable learners and the most able are making excellent progress.

Use teaching assistants well – harness your most expensive resource to make more progress.

Never miss a chance to flag up literacy in every lesson.

Improve questioning quality and let it drive the progress – encourage questions from pupils.

Make assessment responsive so that it informs future planning.

Make feedback specific, developmental and plan it to address individual needs.

Develop independent learning – plan activities that develop habitual self-management and self-confidence in learning.

Create resilience to critical feedback by modelling every mistake as a learning experience.

Create an atmosphere that nurtures the habits of the very best learners – resilience, curiosity and self-regulation.

Create a forum for parents and pupils to feed back their opinions – and make sure you respond to their concerns.

Mindset tweak

Check your own progress using the following grid. Shade where you think you are for each section. Self-evaluate your teaching by looking at your overall score before you get observed, then compare it with the grade an observer gives you.

Teacher _____ Subject _____ Year _____ Set _____ Period _____ Observer _____ Date _____				
	Inadequate	Requires improvement	Good	Outstanding learning and progress (Good, plus ...)	Comments
Start	Takes too long to get the lesson/learning started	Punctual, ordered start. Little reference to prior learning	Punctual, engaging, purposeful start linked to prior learning	Pupils fully engaged and eager from entrance with little input required from the teacher	
Learning outcomes	Not shared and/or not in context and/or ignored in lesson. Low or unrealistically high expectations	Shared and with some sense of context. Expectation not stretching pupils	Shared, engaging, in context and clearly understood by pupils. High, realistic expectations	Outcomes are well planned to convey consistently high expectations of all pupils and are used throughout the lesson to check progress	
Structure	Teacher led, little student input, has no learning outcomes or they are ignored	Rigid structure, has outcomes but not responsive to pupils' needs	Progress checks against outcomes in lesson plan. Flexibility shown in response to student needs	Lesson structure is flexible. The teacher constantly checks progress against outcomes and adjusts the pace and direction in response to individual pupils' needs, delivering outstanding progress	

Range of activities	One approach to learning dominates	Varied learning activities are enjoyed but reflection on their purpose and efficacy may be required	Active learning experiences fully engage and challenge learners to make progress with rigorous review of purpose and efficacy	Imaginative activities fully engage pupils, helping them work very well collaboratively to support each other's learning and progress. They can connect the activities with the learning and the level of achievement
Pace	Slow, laboured, with long periods of pupil inactivity or too fast. Teacher unaware of pupil engagement or learning	The teacher is aware of pupil learning and adjusts plans to suit. However, interventions either slow the pace of learning and/or are unsuccessful	The teacher is aware of how fast to go through the lesson content and when finding pupils in difficulty, quickly and successfully moves them on	A clear sense of pace and challenge helps pupils to work independently and check progress. Pupils find creative solutions and use their own initiative to take control of their own learning progress

Teacher _____ Subject _____ Year _____ Set _____ Period _____ Observer _____ Date _____

	Inadequate	Requires improvement	Good	Outstanding learning and progress (Good, plus ...)	Comments
Subject knowledge	Teachers' subject knowledge insecure and/or there is poor development of subject-specific skills. No growth in pupils' knowledge	Subject knowledge is fairly secure and some learning skills are communicated to pupils. Some growth in pupils' knowledge	Well-developed subject knowledge supports explicit communication of learning process and skills. Good growth in pupils' knowledge	Excellent subject knowledge is delivered and used to plan and assess pupils' skills and development and show links to other learning. Significant growth in pupils' knowledge	
Challenge and differentiation	Particular groups of pupils not identified or teaching fails to cater for them	Groups of pupils and their needs identified. Knowledge and understanding deepened as a result	High expectations of, and appropriately challenging tasks for, all identified pupils. Tasks flexibly adapted to improve individual learning	Teaching shows consistently high expectations of all pupils and challenges all pupils, including the most able and most vulnerable learners, through imaginative, personalised strategies and highly effective interventions	

Teaching assistants	TAs are not prepared before or during the lesson by the teacher. They do the work for the pupils	TAs manage the behaviour of pupils and help them complete work but do not support their learning skills	The TA, with help from the teacher, if required, gives the pupils strategies with which to help themselves	The TAs help pupils by teaching them strategies and learning skills which enable pupils to help themselves make the best progress possible towards the lesson outcomes
Self-assessment	Pupils cannot self-assess against outcomes	Is not rigorous enough to facilitate progress over time	Is regular, consistent, accurately self-critical and shows impact on progress over time	Self-assessment is rigorous, effective and confident with aspirational, realistic target-setting in all aspects of the learning. Pupils can accurately assess their level of achievement
Peer assessment	Pupils are not supportive of each other's progress	Pupils are supportive in assessing each other's work	Pupils are supportive, confident and effective in assessing each other's work	There is evidence of peer assessment helping pupils' skills and knowledge progress in the lesson and over time. Pupils can accurately assess the level of achievement of others against success criteria

| Teacher _____ | Subject _____ | Year _____ | Set _____ | Period _____ | Observer _____ | Date _____ |
| | Inadequate | Requires improvement | Good | Outstanding learning and progress (Good, plus ...) | Comments |

	Inadequate	Requires improvement	Good	Outstanding learning and progress (Good, plus ...)
Questioning	Limited, closed, teacher-led questioning restricted to a few pupils. Inadequately assesses progress towards outcomes	More frequent but often closed with little thinking time and teacher led. Poorly assesses progress towards outcomes. Pupil questions are rare and often poor	Open teacher questions assess progress and uncover misconceptions, promoting flexibility to need. Pupils often ask pertinent questions when they need to	Teacher questioning challenges pupils and encourages metacognition. Pupils have developed questioning skills which help them reflect on their knowledge and understanding of the lesson content and of the learning process itself

Teacher feedback	Cursory, irregular verbal feedback or marking, leaving pupils unaware of what they need to do to progress	Verbal and written feedback helps pupils move forward in their learning	Verbal and written feedback elicits, and shows evidence of, pupil response and action to improve	Verbal and written feedback is regular, personalised and powerful in the way it supports and challenges. Pupils obviously spend a lot of time responding to it. Pupils make rapid gains because of this
Numeracy, literacy, oracy	No planning for numeracy, literacy or oracy. Errors are not challenged or corrected. The teacher commits errors	The teacher models good numeracy, oracy and literacy and corrects pupil errors. Some opportunities taken to develop these in lessons	Numeracy, literacy and oracy skills are discussed and developed within the lesson for all pupils	Frequent opportunities are made available across the curriculum for pupils to demonstrate high levels of numeracy, literacy and oracy. Teaching of them is highly effective

Teacher _____ Subject _____ Year _____ Set _____ Period _____ Observer _____ Date _____

	Inadequate	Requires improvement	Good	Outstanding learning and progress (Good, plus ...)	Comments
Behaviour for learning	Pupils are disengaged, show a lack of respect for each other and/or staff, leading to persistent low-level disruption and tasks remaining unfinished	Inappropriate behaviour is managed but there may be some low-level disruption. Maintaining good conduct is a priority in the lesson	Effective, varied teaching strategies are used which support effective behaviours for learning. Low-level disruption is uncommon	Teaching has cultured pupils who are habitually enthusiastic, active, cooperative and committed learners, with high aspirations and a willingness to discuss and share their learning and their learning strategies	
Progress	Little or no progress is made towards outcomes by the end of the lesson	Most pupils know if they have made progress towards outcomes	Teacher and pupils are clear about what progress has been made and how to address gaps	Progress review is ongoing and engages and is owned by the pupils, who can articulate clearly what they have learned, its context and what they need to do next. As a result, there is evidence of	

				rapid and sustained progress by *all* pupils
Homework	Its purpose is unclear. The response to homework is erratic	Homework is set but fails to properly address learning outcomes and progress towards them. The level of challenge may be insufficient	Homework is linked to outcomes and clearly assesses progress towards them. Pupils are fully engaged and motivated by it	Homework extends the learning journey and provides further open-ended learning opportunities
Grade and comments				**Follow up support plan**

Signed (Teacher) .... Signed (Observer) ....

Source: Adapted from a proforma used at Bridgnorth Endowed School, Shropshire.

Chapter 4

Sustaining your passion and purpose – never stop learning!

Teaching is a wonderful and inspiring job. It can develop into a great career and deliver immense satisfaction and fulfilment. But it can also be very hard work, is highly accountable and is always subject to new demands and expectations. Each time the government changes, there are new initiatives, amendments to the curriculum and waves of platitudes from politicians (who have never, and could never, stand in front of a class full of kids and inspire them) telling us what schools need to do to improve our international standing. It's hard not to become cynical or demotivated when reading the headlines or yet another Ofsted evaluation schedule.

It is also hard not to relax just a little after our NQT year, without a mentor to badger us about our planning and remind us to keep up our learning log. Shaun Allison reflects on his many years leading CPD in a secondary school that teacher's performance can plateau after the intensive early years when frequent monitoring and feedback are provided. After three years or so, a teacher can be tempted to relax and get into a routine of delivering the syllabus and using tried and tested strategies that seem to work. However, this is just the moment when a teacher needs to renew that intensive self-evaluation and check that they are still learning what it means to be the best teacher they can be and that the learning experience for the pupils is continually improving. The new performance management arrangements for teachers will help focus our minds on this.

How can you keep up your enthusiasm for sharpening your skills in today's climate of high-stakes accountability? A world of moving goalposts, where technology is radically changing communication and culture? A world with increasing gaps between the haves and have-nots, the rich and poor, the powerful and the powerless?

Here's how: *you* have the privilege to spend hours in front of young people helping them to develop the learning habits that will prepare them for the challenges ahead. *You* have the power to make a difference for them – no matter what the politicians or Ofsted inspectors do or say. Whatever exam or curriculum changes are made, *you* are the person that sees the children every day and can implement these changes in ways that fit with your own educational principles – the same principles which are the drivers of the growth mindsets outlined in Chapter 1.

Chapter 4

Mindset tweak

Whether you think you can or whether you think you can't – you're right! Believe that no matter what they throw at you, you can help your pupils achieve their potential.

Many changes have taken place under successive governments: specialist schools, academies, literacy and numeracy strategies, computers for schools, interactive whiteboards, revised qualifications, reduction in class sizes, a huge increase in numbers of teaching assistants and the pupil premium.

From this desperate search for the difference that will make the difference, Dylan Wiliam concludes that: 'The only thing that really matters is the quality of the teacher.'[1]

This chapter is about sustaining your energy and passion for teaching over time through:

■ Embracing digital technology and social media.

■ Collaboration – working with and leading colleagues.

■ Coaching yourself and others to thrive in adversity.

---

1   D. Wiliam, 'Teacher Quality: Why It Matters, And How To Get More Of It', *The Spectator* (March 2010). Available at: http://www.dylanwiliam.org/ Dylan_Wiliams_website/Papers.html (accessed 11 September 2013), p. 3.

Embracing digital technology and social media

Teachers have always been in the job of information communication. Now, with the rise of digital media technologies, the means of communicating information are evolving exponentially. I raise various questions in the foreword to Mark Anderson's *Perfect ICT Every Lesson* about the use of ICT in the classroom.[2] How many of us fully use the technology available – not only for the benefit of our pupils, but also for ourselves? How many brilliant lesson ideas have you picked up from Twitter recently? And then delivered using a range of digital media technologies in the classroom?

> There is more processing power in the pocket of your average teenager than was used on the 1969 mission to the moon. In computing, there is a phenomenon called Moore's Law, which states that the number of transistors on integrated circuits doubles approximately every two years. This law has parallels in all aspects of technology – for example, processing speed, memory capacity and pixels in digital cameras are all increasing at an exponential rate.[3]

Teachers who aren't yet using communication devices and social media as learning tools are missing out on amazing learning opportunities. But, at home, their pupils are not!

---

2   M. Anderson, *Perfect ICT Every Lesson* (Carmarthen: Independent Thinking Press, 2013), pp. v–vii.
3   Anderson, *Perfect ICT Every Lesson*, p. 74.

They're filing, sharing, joining, blogging, participating, reviewing, photographing, listening, commenting and observing more often and in more amazing ways than ever before. Many children now grow up with mobile phones, laptops or tablet devices at home – and as soon as they can reach out for them, they begin to play and learn.

Watching 3-year-olds download videos, post photos on their blogs and learn words through their tablet apps, you start to realise that many teachers are delivering lessons that date from a different era. To lead learning today, teachers must be willing to use technology to engage and motivate the young minds already immersed in this new world. This requires a mindset open to pushing ourselves out of our comfort zone and getting excited about trying out new technologies in our classrooms.

We are also entering a brave new world where CPD is radically changing. There are huge learning opportunities available to us through digital media such as Skype, Twitter, blogs linked to TeachMeets and learning forums which are providing a completely new approach to professional development.

There has never been a better time to try new technologies in the classroom and share your successes and challenges with each other in the profession. In his book *Perfect ICT Every Lesson*, Mark Anderson provides lots of ideas to try, whatever the age or stage of our learners.

Flipping your classroom

The idea of flipping your classroom means turning round the traditional way in which pupils work in your lessons. It is a style of 'blended learning',[4] where instead of learning in the classroom and doing homework at home, pupils use technology to learn at home which the teacher then deepens in the classroom. At home, pupils complete (technologically guided) learning activities, making use of materials you have prepared earlier. Often this is done through the use of video clips or other resources that might be placed on your school's VLE,[5] a web channel or other learning platform. It gives a whole new slant on (and hopefully motivation for) 'homework', where pupils are asked to learn new things that will be essential to know for the lesson.

As well as classroom flipping, another fascinating insight from Anderson is the potential for the use of QR codes in lessons. These give us a great opportunity to link to lots of different things online such as:

- Resources that you want pupils to access within your lesson.
- The homework you want pupils to complete – pupils simply scan the QR code to access the text.

---

4 Blended learning is a model which combines face-to-face teaching with technology-mediated activities.
5 Virtual learning environment – there are lots of these available. VLEs are learning platforms where teachers and learners can access, submit, assess and share work across different classes within a whole school.

- A link to any online content that you (or they) have made.
- Links to audio explanations you have saved online alongside resources.
- A rubric that you want pupils to follow – for example, a proofreading code (which could be laminated and stuck to desks in your classroom).

Try this for a thinking skills homework

Teachers often long for stability and consolidation rather than for more change or new initiatives. However, the high-speed world of new technology ensures that this is no longer an option. We all need to react to the world in which our young people live and provide an education that responds to it. At times it may feel risky, but if we do not grasp these new technologies, we risk becoming irrelevant or, even worse, ignored.

Collaboration –
working with and leading colleagues

Interdependence is the highest form of emotional intelligence

When you are working in a school you are part of something very special. In a community that is focused on growing learners, no day is the same, every year group has its own character and – when it's good – there is no better place to be. Wandering out into the playground on duty, chatting to passing pupils about the weather and their homework, catching up with colleagues about their latest strategies with that awkward group in Year 8, watching that shy child excel in the school musical, staying late working on resources for an exciting new cross-curricular project with another teacher, marking those essays in the quiet time before school starts ... and these are just the bits in between teaching five wonderful lessons a day!

But when you reflect on what makes you great at your job, one of the most important aspects is who you work with – and how you learn from your colleagues, be they other teachers, support staff or leaders.

Schools that find laughter typically succeed.

Mick Waters[6]

---

6 Waters, *Thinking Allowed on Schooling*, p. 328.

This has never been more important that in the present climate, according to Wiliam. If we are serious about improving the quality of our education system to meet the demands of the world of work then we need a culture change. No longer can we accept that once one has been teaching for five or ten years, one is 'good to go'. Wiliam suggests that teaching is so complex and challenging that it is only by constantly adapting our strategies and collaborating with others to continuously learn more about what works that we will keep improving. He stresses that we need people drawn to this profession because it is so hard – 'a job so difficult that one's daily experience is of failure, but one where each day, to quote Samuel Beckett one can "fail better"'.[7]

Wiliam also argues that new kinds of teacher learning should involve school-based teacher learning communities, where teachers constantly share, review and build on best practice together. These communities will benefit even further if clusters of schools work together to share practice and resources.

Some of the most successful examples of this type of practice are the current trend in TeachMeets. These are simply meetings of ordinary teachers from one school or a number of schools who get up and present something they have tried for two minutes or ten minutes – with or without visual aids or extensive preparation. The brilliant side effect of this approach is that it models the courage to present to peers and the reflection and review of learning that we are trying to instil in our pupils!

---

7   Wiliam, 'Teacher Quality', p. 6.

> We have been focusing on getting teachers to think their way into new ways of acting, whereas it would be far better to act their way into a new way of thinking.
>
> Dylan Wiliam[8]

Learning forums that discuss more extensive action-based research projects are another way to develop and evolve practice involving particular issues in a school with underperforming groups, phases or subjects. No matter how busy you are, take every opportunity to take part in these – or start them if necessary. If you have any training or CPD, make it your business to try out some of the ideas and make notes in your learning journal about the outcomes.

Take opportunities to work on cross-curricular projects or extra-curricular activities whenever you can because you *always* learn things that improve your practice when working with other people.

Top tip

Share your lesson ideas and resources with others. Give them freely and generously and notice how they are amended and improved by other teachers, then grab them back and use them again. Teachers are magpies and pinching each other's stuff is how we share and learn!

---

8 Wiliam, 'Teacher Quality', pp. 4–5.

Practical ideas for engaging professional development

Some more great ideas schools are using to promote collaborative practice include:

▓ Breakfast swap-shops – where teachers are rewarded with coffee and croissants for bringing in resources before school and sharing them with their colleagues.

▓ Teaching and learning cinemas – show a lesson a month for all to critique and assess using the school observation format. Compare grades and feedback to establish conversations about learning.

▓ Live learning INSETs – where one teacher teaches a group of students in front of *all* staff. Other teachers are then encouraged to critique the lesson in small groups and feed back in the plenary.

▓ Regular TeachMeets for local schools – where all teachers prepare a two-to-seven minute-long presentation about their latest successful (or unsuccessful) strategy, followed by discussion.

▓ A range of mini research projects which *all* departments sign up to – they could be on favourite topics such as feedback, questioning, homework, extended writing or oracy in the classroom. Each project results in a report (one side of A4) on the results of classroom observations against a context of international research which is presented to the staff.

■ Running a master's degree programme at your school for local teachers will encourage research projects that are relevant to your cluster.

Leadership

You are a leader. You lead your class every day, so you have the skills to inspire, the vision to drive forward and the communication skills to enthuse a team.

It is a natural progression to take on a leadership responsibility in a school. Whether it be a pastoral role or subject responsibility, you will love it – if you think you are making a difference. Being brave and ambitious, you may sometimes take on a role that you don't enjoy so much and that takes you too far away from your principles (as discussed in Chapter 1). This is part of your leadership learning journey – a journey that may end up in you becoming a head teacher, a trainer or even an author.

Case study:
leadership that works for teachers and students

Southam College in Warwickshire has improved students' outcomes so that A*–C GCSE grades, including English and maths, have risen from 68% to 89% in three years. The head teacher, Ranjit Samra, says the secret is a relentless focus on the achievement of every individual. A focus which manifests itself in support and challenge, not only for the students, but also for the teachers, teaching assistants and parents. His focus as head teacher has been on persistently building confidence and belief in what can be achieved – staff and pupils wouldn't dare to disagree because of his energy, enthusiasm and courage. I have been his School Improvement Partner for several years, and walking around the school with him meeting the teachers and students in lessons is an inspiration. He leads by example.

Take all the opportunities you can to learn from the best leaders in your school. Accept any challenges offered. Learn everything from the experience and find out where you are happiest in the school system – and don't be afraid to change direction, school, phase or sector, because the best leaders are adaptable, lifelong learners who sometimes get it wrong. Becoming a leader may inspire you in your job. However, if it doesn't, give it a fair try, but don't be afraid to try something else. There is no failure, only feedback.

Case study: developing collaboration and interdependency

Clevedon School, near Bristol has a powerful culture of collaboration that is driving up the performance of teachers and outcomes for children. Walk through the corridors of Clevedon and you will see not only open doors, but teachers eager to share their practice with every visitor and students who are engaged in active research into their own learning.

Some outstanding teachers have been appointed to positions as Learning Associates, working in learning forums and coaching colleagues at different stages of their careers. They conduct coaching observations, giving instant feedback to teachers to encourage them to address underperformance or try new strategies. In addition, they are leading projects on student feedback, digital technology in the classroom, the development of emotionally intelligent teaching, and helping to develop the school as a local centre for innovative CPD. The last TeachMeet attracted 250 people and many more hits on Twitter and YouTube. Eventually, the school plans to run groundbreaking conferences and take a proactive role in creating an exciting creative curriculum that delivers skills that are in demand locally and nationally – as well as continually improving exam outcomes.

Clevedon teachers deliver lessons that are engaging because every objective has the crucial 'so that' element which enables students to understand the success criteria. Lessons are exciting with 'bouncing' questions where different students link ideas and develop their thinking as a class or share kung fu moves to reinforce key terms they need to remember. They listen to each other's extended explanations and comment that teachers 'show me the way' and 'make me think hard'. Able pupils hold forth, teaching their peers and modelling themselves as expert learners. Students self-differentiate and use the SOLO (Structured Observation of Learning Outcomes)[9] project stations to decide what level of learning they are at. Their books show evidence of an evolving new method of feeding back, created by a staff working party, aimed at eliciting a pupil response that will target clearly next moves to make maximum progress.

Some students have been studying the impact of their emotions on learning and chat to the teacher about a graph that showed how various learning situations impacted on outcomes. In a Year 8 drama lesson, students are using iPads to develop scripts and performing their Shakespearean extracts, then ruthlessly evaluating their outcomes against level 6 criteria. The most impressive aspects of their peer and self-assessment was the way they talked about their skills in the language of the subject, demonstrating clear evidence that they were very well aware of progress levels and success criteria.

The leadership of Clevedon are a team who relentlessly pursue a vision of collaboration. There is enthusiasm, passion and endless experimentation – in fact, an obsession with learning, shared by teachers and students alike, and actively promoted by the leadership team. Every term

---

9   For more information on SOLO, visit http://www.johnbiggs.com.au/academic/solo-taxonomy/ (accessed 11 September 2013).

teachers are encouraged to get feedback from their classes, by asking questions such as: 'What do I need to change, keep or grow to help me improve my teaching?' The outcome of this feedback is shared in performance management programmes and school INSET days. It's been a number of years since Clevedon has needed any outside speakers to inspire their staff because teachers are queuing up to share their learning!

Clevedon has now created the ultimate training programme for their staff – The Clevedon Learning Hub CsPD (Continuing self Professional Development). This is a completely personalised training opportunity that offers a wide range of options from the crucial compulsory keynotes to coaching observations, a blogging/tweeting club, TeachMeet opportunities, action research, collaborative planning ... and lots more activities. These are all scheduled at various times of the day and year so that all staff can plan their own continuous learning experience and link it to their performance management.

This is leadership in action led by those who also write about it, such as Jim Smith of the Lazy Teacher series and Zoë Elder, who wrote *Full on Learning*. They are part of the Clevedon leadership team which is headed by inspirational head teacher John Wells.

Coaching yourself and others to thrive in adversity

The hardest thing about being a leader is running a successful team and managing other people's performance. Using a coaching approach enhances collaboration and a genuine sharing of strategies that works for individual teachers – rather than a one-size-fits-all approach to INSET. Coaching can work to deliver high quality teaching and learning for staff and students because it:

- Encourages professional dialogue about improving teaching.
- Helps all teachers understand how to improve their classroom practice step by step.
- Is a bespoke approach and helps individuals to find their own ways to improve.
- Is less prescriptive and more productive in getting teachers to implement policy.
- Can change the mindset and morale of teachers.
- Provides a differentiated tool to support performance management.
- Enhances questioning skills for teachers in the classroom.
- Improves feedback – teacher-to-teacher and teacher-to-pupil.
- Supports metacognitive processes so that teachers can reflect on progress for themselves and see how it works for students.

■ Models how school and classroom leadership works when we appreciate that each pupil and teacher must take ownership of their own improvement.

More information about how to implement coaching effectively in your school can be found in *The Perfect Teacher Coach* by Jackie Beere and Terri Broughton.[10] For coaching to work well, it needs to be embedded as part of the culture of collaboration in the school without making huge time demands on staff. Using a simple coaching model, such as iSTRIDE, means you can have a very focused ten-minute coaching session and elicit a change in behaviour or new solution that can be implemented and evaluated.

The iSTRIDE model

There are many models of coaching available but one that is incredibly useful for schools is the STRIDE model.[11] What follows is an adapted version of the model – iSTRIDE – which is simple, easy to use and implement, yet offers a rigorous and flexible approach.

It is as well to remember that it is only a model: it is not meant to be prescriptive or rigid but organic in nature. With iSTRIDE, coaches can move backwards and forwards along the coaching continuum using a blend of techniques as

---

10 J. Beere and T. Broughton, *The Perfect Teacher Coach* (Carmarthen: Independent Thinking Press, 2013).

11 See W. Thomas, *Coaching Solutions Resource Book* (London: Network Continuum Education, 2005), ch. 2.

appropriate for the coachee. Flexibility and adaptability are always essential to support and meet the coachee's needs.

iSTRIDE is a structured coaching conversation of up to 50 minutes, but it also works well as a powerful ten-minute coaching intervention. It is made up of seven steps as the acronym suggests. These are described in the table below, with examples of useful, non-directive questions for each step supplied later.

Can you see where the coaching conversations you have had in your own workplace would fit into this model?

i	**Information-gathering** Determining the coachee's issues, goals, confidence levels and finding relevant evidence
S	**Strengths** Paying attention to the coachee's strengths and maintaining them in a resourceful mindset
T	**Target/goal-setting** Identifying the target to be achieved and exploring the motivation to achieve it
R	**Resources/reality** Exploring the current situation in relation to the target and identifying limiting beliefs

I	**Ideas/strategies** Seeking ideas that might help achieve the desired target and overcoming limiting beliefs
D	**Decisions** Selecting the most appropriate option from the ideas generated and rehearsing success
E	**Evaluation** There are two parts to this phase: evaluating the solution *now* (exploring a commitment to agree decisions) and evaluating *later* (agreeing a time to follow up on the actions taken arising from the decision)

Adapted with permission from W. Thomas, *Coaching Solutions Resource Book* (London: Network Continuum Education, 2005).

If you look at the following questions, which are tailored to each step of the iSTRIDE model, you can see how using these types of questions with colleagues and in the classroom will encourage ways of thinking that will help others to own their own change and growth.

Guiding beliefs for effective coaching

People already have the resources they need to achieve.

People are always doing their best based on what they know.

Every person is unique.

See people in terms of their potential, not their past performance.

iSTRIDE coaching questions

Information gathering:

Context of the teacher's subject, phase, experience and previous performance

Strengths:

- What have you tried recently that worked?
- What has made you feel successful this week?
- What has been your best achievement of the year?
- What went well this week?
- Tell me about your most sparkling moment as a teacher?
- How does your favourite pupil respond to you?
- What are you most proud of as a teacher?
- When do you perform at your best?

Target/goal:

- What is it you would like to achieve?
- What would need to happen for you to walk away feeling that this is time well spent?
- What exactly is it that will make you feel successful in this?
- What are you building towards?
- What do you really, really want?
- What don't you want?
- What has to happen for you to feel successful?
- How do you know this goal is worth achieving?
- How will you know when you have achieved it?
- What will you see, hear and feel after having achieved it?
- What will achieving this goal do for you/give you?
- How would other people benefit if you reached your goal?
- What is important to you about achieving this goal?
- How much personal control do you have over your goal?
- What can you do yourself to achieve this goal?
- By when do you want to achieve it?
- How will you measure it?
- What is your heart telling you about this dream/goal?
- What is your dream outcome?

Reality:

- Where are you starting from/what have you learnt so far?
- What have you done so far about this dream/goal?
- How effective have your efforts been?
- What's stopped you doing more?
- What have you learnt from what you've done?
- What might you have done differently?
- What insights do you have about yourself/life in general that are relevant to this?
- What will happen if you do nothing?
- What other choices do you have?
- What do you have that you are not using?
- What is holding you back?
- What could stop you achieving your goal?
- What are you afraid of?
- What is not achieving your goal costing you?

Ideas/strategies:

- What could you do?
- What could you do differently from now?
- What must change for you to achieve your goal?
- What approaches have you seen used in similar circumstances?
- Who might be able to help you?

- Who could you learn from?
- What would a wise old friend suggest?
- What would you do if you had ... more/less time, power, money, a magic wand?
- What is the simplest solution?
- What is the right thing to do?
- What is the most courageous step to take?
- If the constraints were removed, what would you do?
- What else could you do ... and what else could you do ... and what else could you do ...?
- What options would you like to act on?
- What could you do that would make the biggest difference?

Decide/commit:

- What is the first logical step?
- What are the next steps?
- Precisely when will you do this?
- What will it cost you if you don't take action?
- What will you gain if you do take action?
- What might get in the way?
- Who needs to know about this?
- What support do you need and from whom?
- How will you get that support?

- Rate on a 1–10 scale your motivation to take the agreed actions.
- What prevents you from being at a 10?
- What do you need to do to get your commitment up to at least 8?

Evaluate:

- What did you do that was different?
- On a scale of 1–10, how hard did you try?
- What was the hardest thing?
- What was the impact (qualitative and quantitative)?
- How did it make you feel?
- What has happened since?
- How have you changed?
- What will you do next?

Self-coaching

The principles and mindsets outlined in Chapter 1 will be key to your surviving and thriving in the teaching profession. In *The Chimp Paradox*, Steve Peters talks of 'the Stone of Life' which clarifies your beliefs and values so you can draw on them in moments of crisis.[12] His 'mind management' metaphor suggests that our emotional brain is like a chimp which can disempower us with self-doubt and anxiety. Peters has

---

12 S. Peters, *The Chimp Paradox: The Mind Management Programme to Help You Achieve Success, Confidence and Happiness* (London: Penguin, 2013), p. 63.

trained the Olympic cycling team and the snooker player Ronnie O'Sullivan to perform at their best using his mind management programme. He suggests the secret of health and happiness is to learn to 'manage' the chimp and 'harness its strength and power'.[13]

We all recognise that irrational thinking can sometimes undermine our performance. We can develop the habits of cynicism, perfectionism or self-flagellation which make us unhappy and stressed. Habitually developing the mindsets outlined in Chapter 1 will help you manage your 'chimp' – and, as a side benefit, you will know just how to help your pupils manage their chimps also!

I call it 'thinking on purpose'. If you allow your default setting to grow undisturbed in your unconscious, before you know it you will find yourself:

▪ Staying late at work.
▪ Saying yes to that extra duty when you mean no.
▪ Finding yourself skipping meetings more often.
▪ Regularly moaning to like-minded miseries in the staffroom about the kids getting 'dumber' and more cheeky.

To avoid this, take time to consciously reflect on your habits and default mindset, and be determined to develop a growth mindset that:

---

13 Peters, *The Chimp Paradox*, p. 8.

- Values the learning journey.
- Is always open to trying new experiences.
- Pushes you out of your comfort zone.

For more on this, see the growth mindset health check (Appendix 1).

Final thoughts

What do I need to do to be the 'perfect' teacher?

Stephen Covey's seminal work on the *7 Habits of Highly Effective People* gave us the insight to question the drivers of our unconscious mind and start to recognise just how we can think on purpose – instead of by accident. This last section of the book brings together all the mindset thinking with the Teachers' Standards[14] to demonstrate the habits you need to develop and what to do to develop them.

---

14 Department for Education, *Teachers' Standards* (London: DfE, 2012).

Embedding the seven habits of highly effective teachers[15]

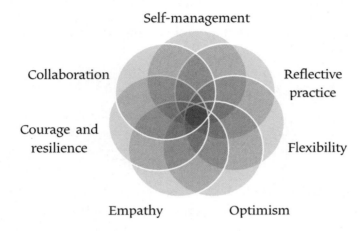

Self-management

Collaboration

Reflective practice

Courage and resilience

Flexibility

Empathy   Optimism

Many of these habits overlap and interact with each other. They are linked to the Teachers' Standards in Appendix 3. Rate yourself out of ten for each of these habits as you read the descriptors below:

Habit 1: Self-management

- Be professional in appearance and behaviour – always.
- Always be punctual to lessons, meetings and completing essential tasks.

---

15 See J. Beere, *The Perfect Ofsted Inspection* (Carmarthen: Crown House Publishing, 2012), p. 16.

- Set 'ruthless priorities'[16] so that everything you do relates to learning and progress. Accept that you may not be able to do everything and may sometimes have to say no to requests.

- Develop resilience so you can bounce back after being given critical feedback from a lesson you (not Ofsted) thought was 'good', or when a normally well-behaved class punishes a less inspiring moment with 'This is so boring' or 'I hate geography'.

- Use stress management strategies – understanding about how the brain works so that when you panic or feel anxious, you realise that it's normal.

- Take care of your mind and body by eating healthy foods, exercising and keeping up to date with research about education.

- Switch off and relax at home. Put the stresses of the day into a box to be retrieved tomorrow and enjoy your partner, kids, pets, TV, garden ...

Schools can promote self-management through a powerful and embedded culture, coaching programme, internal and external training events, celebrations of individual achievements, strict attendance, time-keeping, dress policy and lots of staffroom cream cakes, laughs and social events.

To survive and thrive in teaching, you also have to know when to say no and how to prioritise. You can't just keep adding more to your to-do list. Use your mindset principles

---

16 Azzarello, *Rise*, p. 26.

to provide you with a set of 'ruthless priorities' about what to innovate and what to abandon to become a better teacher. Here are some examples – but make your own list.

Innovate	Abandon
A five-minute lesson plan (see Appendix 1)	Writing out long lessons plans
New learning strategies to try out	Marking that doesn't make a difference
Answering emails immediately and *very* briefly	Time spent writing detailed email responses
Using Twitter and other social media to network for new ideas	Displacement activity such as texting or emailing friends
Skim reading books and magazines, jotting down ideas in a learning log	Being distracted by Facebook photos
Taking part in everything extra-curricular you can manage	Listening to moaners
	Filling in forms
Getting feedback from pupils – formal and informal	Putting up displays (get your artistic students to do it!)
Phoning parents if a child does something good	

Habit 2: Reflective practice – metacognition

Being a reflective practitioner is contagious. The habit of constantly reviewing how you can improve your teaching, and the learning of your class, means you will be flexible and responsive to children's needs. A trainer can easily spot a teaching staff that is habitually reflective. They are self-critical, curious, responsive and take away ideas to play with. They can stand back and analyse why they are responding in certain ways. They love to be challenged in their thinking and often relish the challenge of change. Reflective practitioners can reframe a situation and see it another way and help students do the same. For example, having an inspection means being given a chance to have our performance reflected back to show us how we are doing.

- Keep a learning journal.
- Talk to other teachers about what works and doesn't.
- Post examples of work on the school teachers' blog for review.
- Get feedback from pupils regularly.
- Take part in TeachMeets etc.
- Learn something outside of school.

Habit 3: Flexibility

Adapting to a changing world and ever-changing expectations is an essential habit for students and teachers. A culture that values open-minded approaches to teaching and encourages risk-taking and creativity will encourage flexible approaches to learning. Cross-curricular events, activity weeks, team teaching and a range of opportunities for staff to move outside their comfort zones will ensure they don't get too set in their ways and locked into their subject bunkers.

Flexibility is also developed through personal ownership of change, so coaching used at all levels – as the culture for developing outstanding teaching and learning – will ensure that teachers are constantly prodded to challenge themselves to find their own solutions.

> If you don't embrace the fact that you think about the world in different ways, you severely limit your chances of finding the person that you were meant to be.
>
> Ken Robinson[17]

- Try new ways of working – every week.
- Teach a different subject.
- Always be on the look-out for new jobs and opportunities.
- Talk to new/different people in the staffroom.
- Use Twitter, Facebook, LinkedIn, etc. to extend your contacts and find new ideas to try in the classroom.
- Visit other schools and lessons regularly – just for fun.

---

17 K. Robinson, with L. Aronica, *The Element: How Finding Your Passion Changes Everything* (London: Penguin, 2009), p. 49.

■ Team up with other departments to work together on a theme.

■ Take part in as many extra-curricular activities as you can – especially staff pantos and karaoke.

■ Draw, paint, sing, dance – at whatever level, as often as possible.

■ Coach others and yourself to push yourself out of your comfort zone.

Habit 4: Optimism

There is a four-letter word that is more important for learning than 'exam' and that is 'hope'. Teachers must believe that their pupils can succeed in something. Children have to believe they can succeed in anything and be filled with hope and the expectation that they can make progress. A toddler wakes up every morning believing that he can and will learn new things. He will show a relentless optimism and determination to learn to walk, talk and find out about the world – until he is taught, or learns, to doubt himself and his abilities. Then everyone else starts constructing his learning.

Optimism about learning and having the potential to succeed are contagious. So are pessimism and negativity. There is plenty of research evidence to show that optimism can help us succeed[18] and that creating a culture of optimism and hope in the classroom supports well-being. Some teachers believe

18 See, for example, Martin Seligman's *Flourish: A New Understanding of Happiness, Well-Being – And How to Achieve Them* (London: Nicholas Brealey Publishing, 2011).

that it is important to be realistic rather than optimistic and that it is wrong to raise hopes that children can achieve more than we think they are capable of. But do we know what they are capable of? Have any children gone on to achieve amazing things in working life even though they were a resounding 'failure' at school? Of course they have.

I once delivered an INSET at a school where everyone seemed to have a deeply held belief that any pupil can achieve an A – no matter how long it takes – if we find the right way to teach them. That school had the best value-added results in the country. Having the habit of optimism also helps develop the resilience (see Habit 6) essential for learning so that children can continually reframe failure as an opportunity to learn. Too often we get into the habit of focusing on the bad bits and reliving them over and over again. This is destructive and pointless. When you imagine or remember something your brain experiences it again, reinforcing those feelings – so use this to develop a positive frame of mind. Yes, we have to learn from mistakes, but we can always change what we do to get a different result.

▪ Think of your very best moment of teaching this week. Relive it over and over and enhance the good bits so it is even better.

▪ Reflect and reframe a negative moment with 'What can I learn from this?'

▪ Make a list of all the good things about your class, job or team.

- Keep a 'victory log'[19] which tracks all the good things that happen in your class.

- Challenge negative generalisations such as 'I never get on with Year 8' with 'Which lessons do work well with Year 8?'

- Rehearse your worst lesson by imagining it goes brilliantly – as many times as you can.

- Use mantras that focus on success, such as 'If you think you can or if you think you can't you are right' and 'The harder I work the cleverer I get'.

- Have an optimistic goal you are working towards – you can adapt and adjust it through time.

Habit 5: Empathy

Empathy is part of our natural ability to reflect other people's emotions and thereby understand their perspective on the world. MRI scanning can now detect mirror neurons in our brains that light up when we respond to other people's feelings. This natural tendency to respond to others is the key to altruism and human benevolence. Most teachers go into the profession because they get a kick out of helping others succeed and find nothing more satisfying than turning a challenging class on to learning.

---

19 For more on victory logs see A. Vass, 'The 7 Most Common Mistakes in Classroom Management – and How to Avoid Them!' Available at: http://www.andyvass.net/pdfs/7commonmistakes0112.pdf (accessed 27 September 2013).

There is another reason why empathy is a most important habit for great teachers: empathetic people are great at getting rapport. Rapport is that deep communication with a class or individual that elicits wonderful states of cooperation and motivation. It comes about through an ability to tune in to other people's interests. It's not just about what is said but the way it is said, so body language, intonation, register, eye contact and so on are all part of developing great rapport with a pupil or class. Knowing and understanding what they are interested in and being able to see the world from their viewpoint really helps to get rapport with pupils – or any audience. Teachers who have high levels of empathy can get kids on side and spread the culture of compassion that needs to underpin an 'outstanding' school community.

- Listen closely to feedback so you can adapt your communication.
- Tune in to the people/pupils in front of you by listening to everything they say and understanding their map of the world.
- Don't take bad behaviour personally but try to understand what is motivating them to do it.
- Go to your leaders with ideas and solutions – not moans and problems.

Habit 6: Courage and resilience

Being creative means breaking the rules – finding new solutions and pushing back the boundaries. This takes courage and confidence as it may go wrong – creativity is a risky business. We all have our comfort zones and these are part of our habitual behaviours – like sitting in the same seat in the staffroom, using the same coffee cup, teaching the same scheme of work and talking to the same colleagues. It feels good to be familiar and comfortable, but great teachers enjoy pushing themselves outside their comfort zones and helping students to do the same. You'll know that we all learn best when we are a bit out of our depth and slightly scared. Being ambitious for your classes means having to try new ways of working – particularly for groups of children that don't learn easily.

- Feed your self-confidence through self-disclosure – be honest when you are struggling and seek out help.
- Do the things that scare you the most – public speaking, parachuting, taking assembly, running in the teachers' race …
- Be brave when trying out new strategies – they may not work straight away so there will be some scary moments.
- Seek out feedback from leaders, pupils and parents because that's how you will know how you are doing.
- Have high expectations of yourself but forgive yourself when it goes wrong – as long as you have learnt something.
- Put yourself in the spotlight.
- Always admit when you are wrong and show how you will put it right.

▓ Run a workshop on emotionally intelligent parenting and help parents to develop these habits for themselves and their children.

Habit 7: Collaboration

Human beings were born to collaborate and learn from each other. The very best teachers love to share ideas and resources and find a synergy in the cross-fertilisation of ideas across departments and schools. Whether this is through informal chat, a Twitter forum or attending conferences and subject workshops, being a good collaborator will enhance your teaching. If teachers can develop the habit of collaboration they will pick up the latest thinking, get involved in action research and ensure that kids have transferable skills that make essential connections between subjects. Teachers who collaborate well will lead the general discourse around the school about the vision and values that make it outstanding.

Mentoring, buddying or coaching is essential to embed great learning across the school, so training staff about the importance of collaboration – and rewarding and encouraging it – will make a great difference to the feel of the school. Everything from staff karaoke or pantomimes to regular cross-curricular days and mixed staff INSET encourage great collaboration. We can never underestimate the influence of the 'movers and shakers' in the staff who are very good collaborators and who are always positive and optimistic. They influence the mood of the school. Great collaborators are gold dust. They aren't always heads of faculty, but they are the staff members who organise the school social or quiz night and volunteer to lead twilight INSET when they have been on a course.

- Network in person as often as possible – with different departments, schools, businesses and colleagues in the staffroom and at events.
- Network electronically through Skype and social media formally and informally.
- Work with different departments on INSET day whenever possible.
- Work closely and value support staff, governors and business links – you can learn much from them.
- Mentor a new teacher or coach a colleague – you will learn much about yourself from this process.
- Help with sports day, productions and events for parents.
- Share resources and ideas.
- Organise a staff social event.

And in those moments of weakness ...

What happens when you wake up at 3 a.m. on 31 August thinking, 'I don't know if I can do this anymore'. We have all done it – no one is a hero at 3 a.m. The most important thing to remember is that, if you track through your career, there will always be moments of crisis, moments of success, periods of excitement and anticipation, and long weeks of exhaustion. You will make mistakes and experience failure. Remember, the best teachers constantly learn from and support each other and see their job as a lifelong learning experience. At your best, you are an inspiration, modelling the habits of good learners. At your worst, you are still a learner, acting on feedback – which is still no bad thing!

As a trainer of teachers at all stages of their careers, I am constantly in awe of their dedication and passion, and of their determination to make a difference to the young people they work with. Beyond the next government initiative, change in curriculum or exam syllabus, what really matters is what teachers say and do in classrooms to help learners grow into creative, adaptable, industrious and caring people. Love your job, love the kids and never give up trying to make a difference ... good luck!

Be the change you want to see.

Gandhi

Appendices

Appendix 1
Growth mindset health check

Mark 1–4 or n/a: 1 = Always, 2 = Sometimes, 3 = Rarely,
4 = Never

Do you:	1–4
Believe intelligence is learnable?	
Plan your lessons with opportunities for mistakes as learning opportunities?	
Enjoy new challenges and feel comfortable with change?	
Build in time for thinking and reflecting on the learning process?	
Reward effort rather than just focusing on outcome?	
Give maximum opportunity for pupils to teach/ coach each other?	
Give student choice a high priority in tasks?	

Train your pupils to be assessment literate by understanding how they can make progress?	
Encourage regular self-assessment and goal-setting?	
Train pupils to give high quality peer assessment?	
Vary your lesson structure, classroom layout and pupil groupings regularly?	
Ensure pupils talk (on task) in the lesson more than you do?	
Review and reflect on learning at several points in the lesson, in various ways?	
Insist that pupils make up their own questions and challenges?	
Model risk-taking by challenging yourself to try out new modes of teaching?	
Regularly work with your teaching assistants to try new strategies to help pupils who are not meeting targets make a learning breakthrough?	
Make sure your pupils have a language to talk about their learning and what works or doesn't work for them?	
Relate lessons to their real world to make it relevant to their pupils?	

Focus on intrinsic motivation rather than external rewards?	
Develop the habits of emotional intelligence such as resilience, empathy and optimism in your lessons through metacognition?	
Give effective formative feedback that pupils immediately respond to?	
Ask for feedback from them about how your teaching is working for the pupils?	
Learn from the pupils about social media, technology, etc.?	
Reward creativity and initiative?	
Differentiate by tuning in to the learning needs of everyone and intervening effectively?	
Start each lesson with 'What do you think we need to do now?'	
Answer questions with another question?	
Set learning-to-learn objectives as well as content objectives?	
Connect classroom learning to home, parents, hobbies and the workplace?	
Ensure that you are learning something new outside of teaching every year?	

Total score divided by number of scores =	
1 = Always, 2 = Sometimes, 3 = Rarely, 4 = Never	
Targets:	

Teacher tracking tool for performance management

Teacher Subject			Academic Year	
	Date	Who	Strengths (including grade)	Areas for development
Observations				
Pupil tracking				
Scrutiny of work				
Pupil feedback				
Performance management				

Coaching			
Continuing professional development	Term 1		
	Term 2		
	Term 3		
Overall evaluation		Main development points/next steps	

Note: Adapted from Dawn Burns, Hackleton Primary School, Northamptonshire.

Self-evaluation summary

A. Achievement: Grade			
School Self Evaluation			
Priorities	Personal	School	
Impacts [year] Actuals [year]			

PRIORITY A1:

Impacts/targets:

Action	Specific	Resources and timeframe	Monitoring

Appendix 3

Teaching staff performance review against Teachers' Standards

Teacher: .... **Reviewer:** .... **Date of meeting:** ....

1 = Extraordinary performance, 2 = Met securely, 3 = Making good progress towards, 4 = Not met

Teachers' Standards	Summary of evidence	Judgement
1. Set high expectations which inspire, motivate and challenge pupils		1 2 3 4
2. Promote good progress and outcomes by pupils		1 2 3 4
3. Demonstrate good subject and curriculum knowledge		1 2 3 4

4. Plan and teach well-structured lessons	1	2	3	4
5. Adapt teaching to respond to the strengths and needs of all pupils	1	2	3	4
6. Make accurate and productive use of assessment	1	2	3	4
7. Manage behaviour effectively to ensure a good and safe learning environment	1	2	3	4

Teachers' Standards	Summary of evidence	Judgement
8. Fulfil wider professional responsibilities		1 2 3 4
9. Teachers uphold public trust in the profession and maintain high standards of ethics and behaviour, within and outside school		Met Not met
10. Teachers must have proper and professional regard for ethos, policies and practices of the school in which they teach, and maintain high standards in their own attendance and punctuality		Met Not met

	Met / Not met
11. Teachers must have an understanding of, and always act within, the statutory frameworks which set out their professional duties and responsibilities	

Performance development objectives	Summary of evidence against performance development objectives to meet the Teachers' Standards	Judgement
School objective		Met Good progress towards Not met
Subject objective		Met Good progress towards Not met
Professional objective		Met Good progress towards Not met

Teaching and learning responsibility objective		Met / Good progress towards / Not met
Overall performance against the Teachers' Standards (please tick the appropriate overall level below)		✓
Level 1:	Extraordinary performance	
Level 2:	Met securely	
Level 3:	Majority of Standards met and making good progress towards remaining Standards	
Level 4:	Some Standards met but significant number of Standards are not met	
Level 5:	Not met	

Commentary supporting judgement on overall performance against the Teachers' Standards:

Following this performance development annual review, I recommend/do not recommend the relevant pay progression (please delete as necessary).

Teacher signature .... P.D. Reviewer signature ....

Note: Based on a sample document from Huntington School, Yorkshire.

Appendix 4

Ofsted guidance for judging the quality of teaching and evaluating an outstanding lesson

The most important purpose of teaching is to raise pupils' achievement. Inspectors consider the planning and implementation of learning activities across the whole of the school curriculum, together with teachers' marking, assessment and feedback to pupils. They evaluate activities both within and outside the classroom. They also evaluate teachers' support and intervention strategies and the impact that teaching has on the promotion of pupils' spiritual, moral, social and cultural development.

When evaluating the quality of teaching in the school, inspectors will consider the extent to which:

- The teaching in all key stages and subjects promotes pupils' learning and progress across the curriculum.
- Teachers have consistently high expectations of pupils.

- Teachers improve the quality of learning by systematically and effectively checking pupils' understanding in lessons, and making appropriate interventions.
- Reading, writing, communication and mathematics are well taught.
- Teachers and other adults create a positive climate for learning in which pupils are interested and engaged.
- Marking and constructive feedback from teachers contributes to pupils' learning.
- Teaching strategies, including setting appropriate homework, together with support and intervention, match individual needs.

This is an example of evaluation notes from an outstanding lesson observation.

Evidence

- Rapid engagement in paired activity investigating lesson key concept.
- Teacher quickly established prior learning and level of knowledge to pitch it appropriately.
- Resources enable the students to move on to the tasks without loss of pace, are engaged by the task and motivated to think more deeply.
- Dialogue between teacher and students demonstrates good relationships.

- The resources are appropriate and encourage deeper thinking – students respond by working cooperatively and are enthusiastic about their learning.

- Copying down the learning objectives from the board slows pace.

- A lower ability student is asked to explain the task and this clearly shows an established routine. This works well in ensuring any misconceptions are resolved and that if he understands others probably also do. A very effective strategy!

- Teacher circulates well and asks challenging, open, targeted questions to ensure students are thinking at an appropriate level. He systematically and effectively checks students' understanding of the topic. He uses praise well to motivate students.

- Students clearly enjoy the active learning and find it more engaging. They are articulate about describing how this method helps them to make better progress in their learning.

- On occasions the teacher is too quick to give the answers rather than making them think even more.

- Whiteboard task to assess understanding shows that the majority have grasped the main concept but that some (particularly boys?) still have gaps in their knowledge and understanding of the model. It does not enable the teacher to accurately assess learning and progress of all. Some higher attaining pupils

(HAPs) have answers on display which others could copy.

- Because the teacher links the activity to a final exam-style question the students are able to measure their understanding in real terms. However, Jenny has a target of C and is currently working at A–A* –which paper is she going to be sitting?

- Teacher skilfully uses the examples to explain and model the key features of high quality answers. This works extremely well!

- It is clear that rapid progress has been made on this topic. Teacher double checks the impact on progress by focusing on geographical terminology and connectives and introducing peer assessment/ evaluation – this works very well and is clearly something the students are used to doing over time.

Evidence of SMSC

Some missed opportunities.

Evaluation

Strengths

- A highly practical lesson with a variety of activities that generated high levels of engagement and curiosity which motivated students. This resulted in them making exceptionally good progress.

- The teacher's high expectations and skilful questioning results in excellent progress and deeper thinking/understanding of the topic.
- Rapid progress is made by all students because the teacher carefully planned sequential activities that built on skills and understanding in a lively and exciting way.
- The constructive feedback was of a consistently high quality and motivated the students even further – leading to even higher levels of engagement and interest.

Weaknesses

- Some general questioning was a little closed and gave away answers before students had a chance to work it out.
- Some students' targets were below the grades they were working at – which would need further investigation.[1]

---

1   Adapted from Ofsted, *School Inspection Handbook*. Ref. 120101 (London: Ofsted, 2013).

Appendix 5

Student self-assessment for writing

Level 1	Level 2	Level 3 (E)	Level 4 (D)	Level 5 (C)	Level 6 (B)	Level 7 (A)	Level 8 (A*)	Exceptional performance
I can write simple words and put them together in simple phrases.	I can write simply and what I write makes sense.	I can write stories in the order that they happen (chronologically) and I try to make them interesting and easy to read.	I can write different types of writing (forms), which are interesting to read.	I can write clearly and in an interesting way, which is appropriate for the people I am writing for (the audience) and the reason I am writing (the purpose).	I can write interestingly enough to keep readers interested.	I can use grammar and vocabulary correctly; I can spell complex words correctly; and I can present work neatly and clearly.	I can write in particular ways (e.g. I choose particular words and expressions) to create effects and interest the reader.	I can write in a complex and striking style, and maintain the reader's interest.
I know what a full stop is and I usually know where I should put one in my writing.	I can make what I write interesting and easy to read.	I can change the way I write (style) depending on who I am writing for and why I am writing.	I can alter the way I write when I write for different people and for different reasons.	I can use interesting words correctly and I can spell difficult (complex) words correctly.	I can write in the appropriate style for the purpose. This includes writing in a formal (impersonal) style.	I can describe characters and settings in detail.	I can write stories (narrative) which are well structured and carefully written.	
I can write letters clearly and usually correctly.	I can usually use full stops and capital letters.	I can arrange ideas in an order so they make sense.	I can choose interesting words to make my writing more interesting.	I can use commas, paragraphs, apostrophes and speech marks correctly.	I can choose words (vocabulary) and write sentences in particular ways to create effects.	I can organise ideas and information carefully so it is understandable (coherent).	I can write non-fiction which is coherent and clear.	
	I can spell short, simple words correctly.	I can use a lot of different and interesting words and I usually write sentences which make sense (are grammatically correct.)	I can write long sentences correctly; I spell longer words correctly; and I can use punctuation, including commas, correctly.	I can write clearly in a joined-up (cursive) style.	I can spell complex words correctly.	I can choose an appropriate style for what I am writing.	I can choose vocabulary and grammar very carefully to convey exactly what I mean.	
	When I can't spell a word I try to spell it the way that it sounds.	I can use full stops, capital letters and question marks correctly.	I can write neatly and so it is readable.		I can use punctuation correctly.	I can use paragraphs and punctuation to make what I am writing about easier to follow and understand (coherent).	I can use punctuation and paragraphing.	
	I can join up some words when I write.	I can usually spell longer words correctly.			I can organise ideas into separate paragraphs.			
		I can use joined-up writing which is easy to read.						

Level 1	Level 2	Level 3 (E)	Level 4 (D)	Level 5 (C)
I can write simple words and put them together in simple phrases.	I can write simply and what I write makes sense.	I can write stories in the order that they happen (chronologically) and I try to make them interesting and easy to read.	I can write different types of writing (forms), which are interesting to read.	I can write clearly and in an interesting way, which is appropriate for the people I am writing for (the audience) and the reason I am writing (the purpose).
I know what a full stop is and I usually know where I should put one in my writing.	I can make what I write interesting and easy to read.	I can change the way I write (style) depending on who I am writing for and why I am writing.	I can alter the way I write when I write for different people and for different reasons.	I can use interesting words correctly and I can spell difficult (complex) words correctly.

Level 6 (B)	Level 7 (A)	Level 8 (A*)	Exceptional performance
I can write interestingly enough to keep readers interested.	I can use grammar and vocabulary correctly; I can spell complex words correctly; and I can present work neatly and clearly.	I can write in particular ways (e.g. I choose particular words and expressions) to create effects and interest the reader.	I can write in a complex and striking style, and maintain the reader's interest.
I can write in the appropriate style for the purpose. This includes writing in a formal (impersonal) style.	I can describe characters and settings in detail.	I can write stories (narrative) which are well structured and carefully written.	

Level 1	Level 2	Level 3 (E)	Level 4 (D)	Level 5 (C)
I can write letters clearly and usually correctly.	I can usually use full stops and capital letters.	I can arrange ideas in an order so they make sense.	I can choose interesting words to make my writing more interesting.	I can use commas, para-graphs, apostro-phes and speech marks correctly.
	I can spell short, simple words correctly.	I can use a lot of different and interesting words and I usually write sentences which make sense (are grammati-cally correct.)	I can write long sentences correctly; I spell longer words correctly; and I can use punctua-tion, including commas, correctly.	I can write clearly in a joined-up (cursive) style.

Level 6 (B)	Level 7 (A)	Level 8 (A*)	Exceptional performance
I can choose words (vocabulary) and write sentences in particular ways to create effects.	I can organise ideas and information carefully so it is understandable (coherent).	I can write non-fiction which is coherent and clear.	
I can spell complex words correctly.	I can choose an appropriate style for what I am writing.	I can choose vocabulary and grammar very carefully to convey exactly what I mean.	

Level 1	Level 2	Level 3 (E)	Level 4 (D)	Level 5 (C)
	When I can't spell a word I try to spell it the way that it sounds.	I can use full stops, capital letters and question marks correctly.	I can write neatly and so it is readable.	
	I can join up some words when I write.	I can usually spell longer words correctly.		
		I can use joined-up writing which is easy to read.		

Level 6 (B)	Level 7 (A)	Level 8 (A*)	Exceptional performance
I can use punctuation correctly.	I can use paragraphs and punctuation to make what I am writing about easier to follow and understand (coherent).	I can use punctuation and paragraphing.	
I can organise ideas into separate paragraphs.			

References and further reading

Alfieri, L., Brooks, P. J., Aldrich, N. J. and Tenenbaum, H. R. (2011) 'Does Discovery-Based Instruction Enhance Learning?' *Journal of Educational Psychology* 103(1): 1–18.

Allison, S. (in press) *The Perfect CPD*. Carmarthen: Independent Thinking Press.

Anderson, M. (2013). *Perfect ICT Every Lesson*. Carmarthen: Independent Thinking Press.

Azzarello, P. (2010) *Rise*. Palo Alto, CA: Ten Speed Press.

Barber, M. and Mourshed, M. (2007). *How the World's Best Performing School Systems Come Out On Top*. London: McKinsey & Company.

Beadle, P. (2010) *How to Teach*. Carmarthen: Crown House Publishing.

Beere, J. (2007) *The Learner's Toolkit*. Carmarthen: Crown House Publishing.

Beere, J. (2010) *The Primary Learner's Toolkit*. Carmarthen: Crown House Publishing.

Beere, J. (2012) *The Perfect Ofsted Inspection*. Carmarthen: Crown House Publishing.

Beere, J. (2012) *The Perfect Ofsted Lesson*. Carmarthen: Crown House Publishing.

Beere, J. and Broughton, T. (2013) *The Perfect Teacher Coach*. Carmarthen: Independent Thinking Press.

Churches, R. and Terry, R. (2007) *NLP for Teachers: How to Be a Highly Effective Teacher*. Carmarthen: Crown House Publishing.

Covey, S. R. (1998) *The 7 Habits of Highly Effective Families*. London: Simon & Schuster.

Curran, A. (2008) *The Little Book of Big Stuff about the Brain*. Carmarthen: Crown House Publishing.

Department for Education (2012). *Teachers' Standards*. London: DfE.

Department for Education and Skills (2007) *Assessment for Learning 8 Schools Project Report*. London: DfES.

Didau, D. (2012) *The Perfect Ofsted English Lesson*. Carmarthen: Independent Thinking Press.

Duhigg, C. (2012) *The Power of Habit: Why We Do What We Do and How to Change*. London: William Heinemann.

Dweck, C. (2006) *Mindset: The New Psychology of Success*. New York: Random House.

Elder, Z. (2012) *Full On Learning: Involve Me and I'll Understand*. Carmarthen: Crown House Publishing.

Gadsby, C. (2012) *Perfect Assessment for Learning*. Carmarthen: Crown House Publishing.

Gilbert, I. (2007) *The Little Book of Thunks: 260 Questions to Make Your Brain Go Ouch!* (Independent Thinking Series). Carmarthen: Crown House Publishing.

Gilbert, I. (2010) *Why Do I Need a Teacher When I've Got Google?* London: Routledge.

Gladwell, M. (2008) *Outliers: The Story of Success.* London: Penguin.

Goleman, D. (1996) *Emotional Intelligence: Why It Matters More Than IQ.* London: Bloomsbury.

Gregory, S. (2012) National Director Education and Early Years Introduces the Schools Report 2011/12 [video transcript] (27 November). Available at: http://www.ofsted.gov.uk/resources/ofsted-annual-report-201112-susan-gregory-national-director-education-and-early-years-introduces-sch (accessed 27 September 2013).

Hattie, J. (2012) *Visible Learning for Teachers: Maximizing Impact on Learning.* London: Routledge.

Higgins, S., Kokotsaki, D. and Coe, R. J. (2011) *Toolkit of Strategies to Improve Learning: Summary for Schools Spending the Pupil Premium.* London: Sutton Trust.

Hook, P. and Vass A. (2000) *Confident Classroom Leadership.* London: David Fulton.

Jensen, E. (1995) *The Learning Brain.* San Diego, CA: Turning Point.

Kahneman, D. (2012) *Thinking, Fast and Slow.* London: Penguin.

Lang, J. M. (2013) *Cheating Lessons: Learning from Academic Dishonesty*. Cambridge, MA: Harvard University Press.

Ofsted (2013) *The Framework for School Inspection*. Ref: 120100. London: Ofsted.

Ofsted (2013) *School Inspection Handbook*. Ref 120101. London: Ofsted.

Ofsted (2013) *Subsidiary Guidance*. Ref: 110166. London: Ofsted.

Peters, S. (2013) *The Chimp Paradox: The Mind Management Programme to Help You Achieve Success, Confidence and Happiness*. London: Penguin.

Robinson, K. with Aronica, L. (2009) *The Element: How Finding Your Passion Changes Everything*. London: Penguin.

Rowling, J. K. (2008) 'The Fringe Benefits of Failure and the Importance of Imagination'. Commencement Address at the Annual Meeting of the Harvard Alumni Association.

Seligman, M. (2011) *Flourish: A New Understanding of Happiness, Well-Being – And How to Achieve Them*. London: Nicholas Brealey Publishing.

Smith, J. (2010) *The Lazy Teacher's Handbook: How Your Students Learn More When You Teach Less* (Independent Thinking Series). Carmarthen: Crown House Publishing.

Thomas, W. (2005) *Coaching Solutions Resource Book*. London: Network Continuum Education.

Vass, A. (n.d.) 'The 7 Most Common Mistakes in Classroom Management – and How to Avoid Them!' Available at:

http://www.andyvass.net/pdfs/7commonmistakes0112.pdf (accessed 27 September 2013).

Wall, K., Hall, E., Baumfield, V., et al., (2010) *Learning to Learn in School Phase 4 and Learning to Learn in Further Education*. London: Campaign for Learning. Available at: http://www.campaign-for-learning.org.uk/cfl/learninginschools/projects/learningtolearn/news/casestudies/index.asp (accessed 11 September 2013).

Waters, M. (2013) *Thinking Allowed on Schooling*. Carmarthen: Independent Thinking Press.

West Burnham, J. and Coates, M. (2006) *Transforming Education for Every Child: A Practical Handbook*. London: Network Educational Press.

Wiliam, D. (2010) 'Teacher Quality: Why It Matters, And How To Get More Of It', *The Spectator* (March). Available at: http://www.dylanwiliam.org/Dylan_Wiliams_website/Papers.html (accessed 11 September 2013).

Useful Twitter addresses to follow

@ColinGoffin

@DeputyMitchell

@DKMead

@educationCPD

@fullonlearning

@headguruteacher

@HuntingEnglish

References and further reading

@ICTEvangelist

@jackiebeere

@johntomsett

@LearningSpy

@musicmind

@Pekabelo

@RealGeoffBarton

@SLTchat

@TeacherToolkit

@tesResources

@ThatIanGilbert

@ThisIsSethsBlog

@tombennett71

@Totallywired77

978-178135130-7

978-178135137-6

www.independentthinkingpress.com

978-178135136-9

978-178135125-3

www.independentthinkingpress.com

978-178135103-1

978178135104-8

 www.independentthinkingpress.com

978-178135090-4

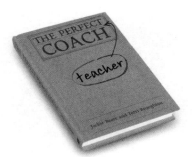

978-178135003-4

www.independentthinkingpress.com

978-178135052-2

978-178135002-7

www.independentthinkingpress.com

978-178135088-1

978-178135000-3

![i] www.independentthinkingpress.com